POLICY STUDIES IN EMPLOYMENT AND WELFARE NUMBER 1

General Editor: Sar A. Levitan

Programs in Aid
of the Poor for the 1980s

Fourth Edition

Sar A. Levitan

The Johns Hopkins University Press, Baltimore and London

This study was prepared under a grant from the Ford Foundation.

The Johns Hopkins University Press, Baltimore, Maryland 21218
The Johns Hopkins Press Ltd., London

Library of Congress Cataloging in Publication Data

Levitan, Sar A.
Programs in aid of the poor for the 1980s.

(Policy studies in employment and welfare; no. 1)
Bibliography: p.
Includes index.
1. Public welfare—United States.   2. Economic assistance, Domestic—United
States.   I. Title.
HV95.L54   1980   362.5'8'0973   80-8093
ISBN 0–8018–2483–4
ISBN 0–8018–2484–2 (pbk.)

Contents

Preface to the Fourth Edition

Programs in Aid of the Poor was originally prepared in 1965 for the National Commission of Technology, Automation, and Economic Progress and was published simultaneously by the commission, as part of its studies, and by the W. E. Upjohn Institute for Employment Research. The initial intention merely to update the study in 1969 became a complete revision reflecting the radical changes brought about in the American welfare system by the Great Society. Contrary to the popular image, the first Nixon administration continued to expand the earlier efforts in aid of the poor. But new initiatives have been halted under the succeeding Ford and Carter administrations, although progress on many fronts continued. As the nation entered its third century, other pressing matters slowed the expansion of the welfare state. The present edition represents, therefore, more an updating of developments and operations of expanded old efforts on behalf of the poor than an examination of new initiatives.

The purpose of this study is to review and appraise existing programs in aid of the poor and to explore feasible approaches to the alleviation of poverty in the future. After examining the characteristics of the poor, the study summarizes the major antipoverty measures now in effect, focusing on the operation of the federal welfare system. The system is divided into four types of programs: income maintenance programs aimed largely at aiding the poor who are outside the work force; programs supplying goods and services; programs whose immediate goal is to avert the spread of poverty to new generations; and programs to aid the working poor. The final chapter is devoted to a discussion of programs that might be adopted over the immediate years ahead.

A *caveat emptor* is in order. This study used various estimates of federal funds allocated to the poor. At present, there is no single agency that maintains such numbers, and even programs targeted to help the poor tend to aid nonpoor people also. The estimates presented in this volume were culled from diverse sources and are intended to indicate rough magnitudes of outlays and trends over time rather than data based on rigorous and hard information.

The reader seeking source materials is invited to turn to the suggested readings at the end of each chapter. The excessive references to my other studies are not because they are the "best," but because *Programs in Aid of the Poor for the 1980s* is based on these studies and they offer the inquiring reader convenient sources of the materials used in the present volume.

I am indebted to Susan Appleman, Richard S. Belous, and Clifford Johnson for their assistance in updating this volume. Cathy Glasgow and Nancy Kiefer prepared the volume for publication.

The study was revised under an ongoing grant from the Ford Foundation to the Center for Social Policy Studies of the George Washington University. In accordance with the foundation's practice, complete responsibility for the preparation of the volume was left to the author.

Sar A. Levitan
Center for Social Policy Studies
The George Washington University

Programs in Aid of the Poor for the 1980s

1

The Poor: Dimensions and Programs

If all the afflictions of the world were assembled on one side of the scale and poverty on the other, poverty would outweigh them all.
—Rabba, Mishpatim 31:14

INCOME INEQUALITY

"The poor shall never cease out of the land," according to the Bible. Rather than being a pessimistic forecast, this prophecy is recognition that each society defines poverty in its own terms.

Poverty is a relative concept. It is primarily for this reason that in the richest country in the world, one person in eight can be designated as poor. In less affluent countries, poverty is equated with living at the brink of subsistence. In this country, even the lowest-income families are rarely confronted with the specter of starvation, though many are the victims of an inadequate diet.

Inequality is a problem in all societies at all times. No system distributes income evenly, nor necessarily should it. The reasons for this inequality of income are many. Some are worthy and some are unconscionable, but the trends are remarkably constant. Income distribution today is little different from the pattern just after World War II. The poorest 20 percent of all families receive only about one-third the money income of the top 5 percent, and there is some evidence that these figures may actually understate the full extent of inequality.

1

MEASURING POVERTY

Insofar as it can be measured, poverty can be defined as a lack of goods and services needed for an "adequate" standard of living. Because standards of adequacy vary with both the society's general level of well-being and public attitudes toward deprivation, there is no universally accepted definition of individual or family basic needs. The amount of money income necessary to provide for any agreed-upon set of basic needs is equally difficult to determine. For example, government programs such as free education, subsidized food, or medical care reduce the amount of cash required to support a family; and differentials in the cost of living between urban and rural areas, and among regions, raise the income requirements for some people and lower them for others. It is no wonder, then, that experts differ over the purchasing power that an individual or family needs for a minimum acceptable level of economic welfare.

Despite these conceptual and technical problems of measurement, the federal government has devised a poverty index that has gained wide acceptance. Developed by the Social Security Administration in 1964, this index is based on the cost of a minimum diet, estimated by the Department of Agriculture on the basis of a 1955 survey at about $1.71 per person per day in a four-member family with two school-age children (1979 prices). The total cost of living of the low-income family is estimated to be three times its food expenditures (with adjustments for changes in the level of consumer prices); thus, a larger family will have a proportionately higher poverty threshold. Farm families are presumed to need only 85 percent of the cash income required by nonfarm families, two-person families with an elderly head 10 percent less than those under 65 years of age, and households headed by females slightly less than other households. A summary of the federal government's definition of poverty income, based on 1979 prices, is presented in the following table:

Number of family members	Nonfarm	Farm
1	$3,800	$3,200
2	5,000	4,200
3	6,200	5,300
4	7,500	6,300
5	8,700	7,400
6	9,900	8,500

There are several flaws in this poverty index. First, the distinction between "nonfarm" and "farm" is extremely crude. It makes no allowance for regional variations in the cost of living or for higher prices in central cities, where many of the poor are concentrated. Set initially at 70 percent, the level for farm families was arbitrarily raised to the present level of 85 percent. Second, the food costs on which the budget is based were developed for "temporary or emergency use" and are inadequate for a permanent diet. For a family of four, an annual income of $7,500 (1979 prices) provides only the barest subsistence. Also, the emphasis on cash income alone may yield paradoxical results. Because the income source is not a consideration, the poverty standard excludes persons or families whose cash income is above the poverty threshold, but whose disposable income after Social Security taxes and work expenses are deducted is below the poverty line. On the other hand, a family of four receiving only welfare payments of the same amount or more during the year would not be poor. The exclusion of in-kind benefits and assets in determining the number of poor further detracts from the precision of the index. Nearly 1 of every 11 persons in the United States, mostly poor persons, received food stamps in 1980. Finally, the assumption that a family needs two dollars for shelter, clothing, and other needs for every food dollar (thus a poverty index three times the food budget) was based on the finding that in the 1950s the average consumer spent one-third of his income for food. More recent data indicate that this proportion has fallen to 25 percent, so the food budget might well be multiplied by 4, instead of 3, to derive the poverty level. A poverty line obtained in this way would be considerably higher than the "official" one. The pitfall of using a "stagnant" poverty level—one that adjusts only for price increases but not for productivity gains and the rising living standards of the American people—is also illustrated by the growing gap between the poverty level and median family income. The former doubled between 1960 and 1978, while the latter more than tripled. In 1960 the median family income was 1.9 times the poverty level for a family of four. By 1978 it was 2.8 times as much.

A proposed solution is a flexible poverty line. One suggestion is to divide the median family income by two, thereby pegging the standard for a family of four at two-fifths higher than the level set by the government. Because there has been little redistribution of income in

3

recent years, a flexible index would indicate that our progess against poverty has been scant. For the present, however, the government poverty index is the most widely accepted and workable measure of poverty, and available data are gathered on this basis.

IDENTIFYING THE POOR

Measured by government statistics, poverty declined markedly in the decade of the 1960s. In 1960 nearly 40 million persons, or 22 percent of the population, were classified as poor by the government's poverty index. By 1969, this number had been reduced to approximately 24 million, or 12 percent of the population. Most of this progess occurred during the second half of the decade, when jobs were plentiful. The government-mounted special efforts to reduce poverty also helped. But during the 1970s no apparent headway was made, and in 1978 the number of poor was still 24.5 million (figure 1). Without government welfare payments, it is estimated that 16 percent of this population, instead of 11 percent in 1978, would be living below the poverty level. As noted earlier, the official poverty count ignores the in-kind aid received by the poor. If the value of in-kind assistance had been included, the number of poor would have shown a further sharp decline in 1970s to 8 percent of the population. Still the problem of poverty persists, and the nation's increasing affluence makes the deprivation of those who remain poor both more noticeable and more poignant.

The incidence of poverty is related to age, color, sex of family head, work status, and educational attainment (table 1). Blacks are four times as likely as whites to be poor. Families headed by women are six times as likely to be poor as families headed by males. When the head of the family has eight years of schooling or less, the incidence of poverty is six times that for families headed by a person with some college education.

Overall changes in the number of poor mask the considerable movement of persons into and out of poverty (figure 2). That the total number of poor was slightly lower in 1969, for example, than in 1968, was the net effect of the movement out of poverty by 37 percent of the poor in that year, while 34 percent of those classified as poor in 1969 were not in poverty during the previous year. A longitudinal study of

Figure 1 Poverty, 1960–78

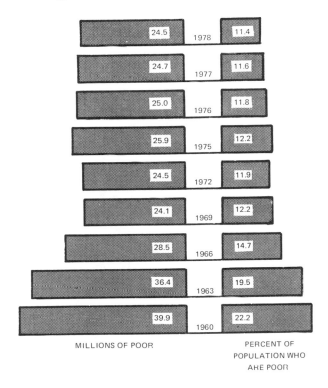

	MILLIONS OF POOR		PERCENT OF POPULATION WHO ARE POOR
1978	24.5		11.4
1977	24.7		11.6
1976	25.0		11.8
1975	25.9		12.2
1972	24.5		11.9
1969	24.1		12.2
1966	28.5		14.7
1963	36.4		19.5
1960	39.9		22.2

SOURCE: U.S. Bureau of the Census

5,000 families by the University of Michigan Survey Research Center found that over a six-year period only one in four of all poor families was counted as poor during the entire period. Over a nine-year period only one in eight remained poor during the entire period. On the other hand, the study revealed that poverty was more pervasive than it appears when looking at one-year poverty figures. Over one-fourth of the population was poor in at least one of the years under study. Blacks, who accounted for 41.3 percent of poor individuals in the sample for 1975, were 77.0 percent of those who were poor throughout the nine-year period. Conversely, more favored

5

Table 1. Characteristics of the poor, 1978

Characteristics	Persons in Families		Persons Living Alone	
	Number (thousands)	Poor as percentage of total in category	Number (thousands)	Poor as percentage of total in category
Total	*19,062*	*10*	*5,435*	*22*
Age Group[1]				
Under 18	9,722	—	—	16
18 to 64	11,542	—	—	7
65 and over	3,233	—	—	14
Race of family head				
White	3,523	7	4,209	20
Spanish origin	559	20	264	30
Black	1,622	27	1,132	39
Other	135	14	94	32
Family status				
Head	5,280	9	5,435	22
Related children	9,722	16	—	—
Others	4,059	6	—	—

Type of residence			
Central city	7,191	14	2,094	21
Outside central city	4,386	6	1,419	17
Farm	857	12	54	14
Other nonmetropolitan	6,628	12	1,868	31
Sex of family head				
Male	2,626	5	1,824	17
Female	2,654	31	3,611	26
Work experience of family head				
Full-year, full-time	849	2	229	3
Part-time or part-year	1,740	16	1,787	28·
Did not work	2,657	24	3,149	39
Armed forces	35	5	0	0
Education of family head, age 25 or over				
8 years or less	1,651	17	1,971	39
1–3 years high school	1,091	14	781	29
4 years high school	1,216	7	805	15
College, 1 year or more	612	3	569	8

[1]These data are not broken down for persons living in families and persons living alone.

Source: U.S. Bureau of the Census

Figure 2 Movement into and out of poverty

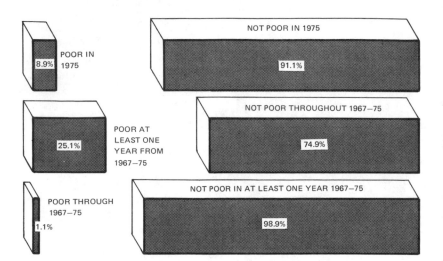

SOURCE: University of Michigan Survey Research Center
NOTE: The percentage of poor families as reported by the Survey Research Center differs from the Current Population Survey data presented in figure 1.

groups, such as whites and male-headed families, comprised a higher proportion of the transitory poor.

For the purpose of this survey, the poor can be divided into four major groups: the elderly, working-age adults who are employed, those of working age who are not employed, and children in poor families. While these groups share the symptoms of low income, their problems vary, and different programs are required to lift them out of poverty.

The Aged Poor

The incidence of poverty remains highest among aged persons. One in every seven persons aged 65 or older lives in poverty, compared with one in nine persons under the age of 65. If anything, the situation may have been worse than these figures indicate, for the estimate of 3.2 million elderly poor excludes many living in public homes and others whose own income would have classified them among the poor but who lived in nonpoor households. There has been a dramatic drop in the number of aged poor—from 4.3 million in 1971 to 3.2 million in 1978. Credit is due largely to more generous social security benefits and the growth of private and veterans' pensions. The Supplemental Security Income program, begun in 1974 and not reflected in these data, may help further reduce the number of aged poor in the future. However, as the aged become more numerous in our society, the problems of meeting their income needs will intensify.

The major cause of poverty among the elderly is that few hold jobs. While some of the elderly poor are willing and able to work regularly, the vast majority cannot do so. Their infirmities are doubly critical because an increasing number of elderly persons live alone and must provide for their own, support. The best and frequently the only way to help these people is through income support. Provision must also be made for high medical costs, which can be devastating for anyone living close to or below the poverty line.

Children in Poverty

At the other end of the age spectrum, one of every three persons classified as poor in 1978 was a child under sixteen years of age, and one child in six lived in poverty. This fact is of special social concern because these children are almost inevitably denied opportunities from the very start and are thus impeded in preparing themselves for productive adult lives.

Many children live in poverty because they are its cause. That is, low-income families are frequently driven into poverty by the addition of family members. There is a close relationship between family size and poverty, with 57 percent of poor children coming from families with five or more members (figure 3). A higher incidence of poverty among larger families is to be expected in a society where need is ignored as a factor in wage determination, and where the necessity of child care often hinders the wife or female family head from earning needed income.

Poor children have special needs over and above those that can be provided by family income maintenance. Health care, compensatory education, and vocational training, in particular, are required to provide permanent exits from poverty.

Figure 3 Poverty and family size, 1978

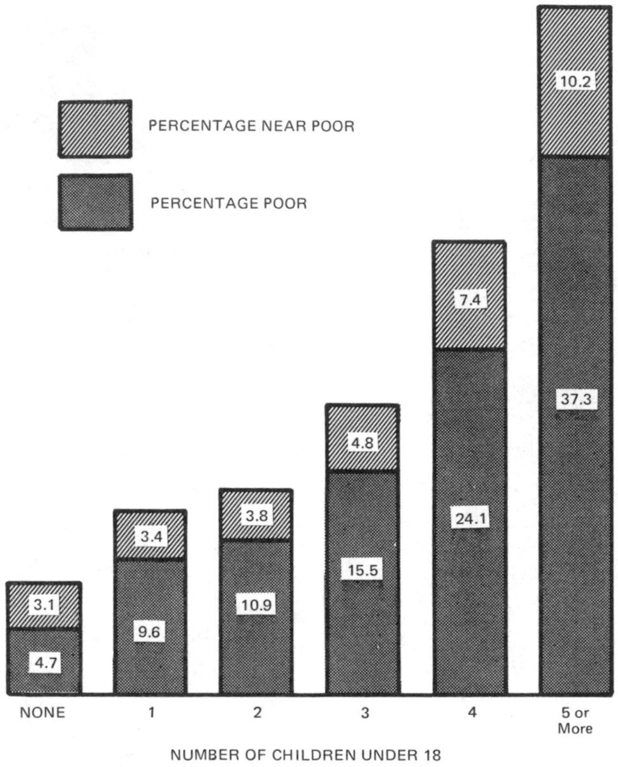
PERCENTAGE NEAR POOR
PERCENTAGE POOR
3.1
4.7
3.4
9.6
3.8
10.9
4.8
15.5
7.4
24.1
10.2
37.3
NONE
1
2
3
4
5 or More
NUMBER OF CHILDREN UNDER 18

SOURCE: U.S. Bureau of the Census

The Working Poor

Lack of employment is often the cause of poverty, but employment itself does not guarantee an adequate income. Close to half of the 5.2 million poor family heads worked in 1978. Many single poor persons under 65 years of age were employed at least part time. For all these persons and their families, poverty was the result of low-paying jobs as well as intermittent unemployment and large families.

Though the problem is often overstated, unemployment remains a major cause of poverty. The poor are the victims of forced idleness more frequently than the nonpoor. Poor family heads, both male and female, are about three times as likely to be unemployed as are nonpoor family heads.

The majority of the working poor who do not experience unemployment encounter other labor market difficulties. Many leave the work force either voluntarily or because of illness or disability. An even greater number are employed at low-paying jobs. One-sixth of all family heads who worked in 1978 were employed primarily as private household or other service workers, laborers, or farmers, but these occupations accounted for 43 percent of the working poor family heads. At least one family head in seven employed in these occupations was in poverty. Close to one-half of poor family heads and over one-third of single poor persons worked during 1978 but were not able to overcome poverty. About one-fifth of all poor families, in fact, had two or more persons working at some time during the year but remained poor. The number of family heads who worked full time year-round but remained poor declined steadily during the 1960s, and at a faster rate than the decrease in the total poverty population. But in 1978 there remained 849,000 family heads, with about 4 million dependents, and another 229,000 unrelated individuals who were continuously employed full-time but were still unable to work their way out of poverty.

For the working poor, then, the problems are frequent joblessness, low wages, and inadequate skills, all of which make the higher-paying jobs inaccessible. Employment and training programs designed to smooth the operation of the labor market, enhance the productivity of low-income workers, and open opportunities for employment and advancement will alleviate the plight of the working poor. Effective enforcement of protective legislation to eliminate discrimination is also required while these employment and training programs are being implemented.

The Nonworking Poor

Despite canards about the link between laziness and poverty, most of the unemployed working-age poor are simply not employable, either because of personal handicaps or because not enough jobs are available for them. Recent data on the reasons that poor people do not work indicate that illness and family responsibilities are the primary barriers. Of poor males aged 22 to 59 who did not work at all during

1978, more than half were ill or disabled. For male family heads, the percentage was probably higher. One out of every two females in this age group cited home responsibilities as the obstacle to outside work, and almost one in five was ill or disabled. Thus, the presence of children not only increases income needs and the likelihood of poverty, but also hinders the employment of mothers and therefore reduces (or limits) the income available to meet family needs. Others were enrolled in school or training programs that would presumably enhance their employability, or had searched unsuccessfully for work. Some of the nonworking poor could and should be lured or goaded into employment; but for the vast majority of these poor, jobs alone are not the answer, and some form of income support must be devised to help them escape deprivation.

STRATEGIES FOR HELPING THE POOR

Poor people need money. Whether they are young or old, their major immediate problem is the lack of income to purchase the most basic goods and services. But beyond this, the various categories of the poor have different needs, many of which cannot be filled with liberalized income-support programs. Family heads and young people with their life's work ahead of them must have not only mere daily subsistence but also encouragement and support for acquiring the skills sought by employers. For the aged, medical care and nursing homes are primary concerns. Children also need health care and the basic education to assure them opportunities in the future. For all poor people, direct provision of housing, medical care, food and other goods and services can serve as a supplement to income maintenance.

Since the time of the New Deal, the United States has developed an intricate, though far from comprehensive, series of programs to assist the economically disadvantaged. The underlying assumption of this system is that special-purpose programs are required to take care of the diverse needs of the poor. Though some programs single out one of the four categories of the poor for special attention, other programs overlap in their coverage. It is easier, therefore, to classify the programs according to what they provide than by the groups they serve.

Types of Programs

Four types of programs are designed to aid the poor: (1) cash support, (2) direct provision of necessities such as food, shelter, and medical care, (3) preventive and compensatory efforts for children and youth, and (4) attempts to restructure existing institutions or to help individuals adapt to those institutions.

Income maintenance programs are the major form of assistance to the poor. Because poverty is generally defined as the lack of adequate income, it can most directly be attacked by cash subsidies. To the extent that the family unit itself is the best or at least the most appropriate judge of how its limited resources should be allocated, income maintenance is a more acceptable form of assistance than the provision of goods and services.

The income subsidy approach is not without its inherent problems, however. The probability that under *current* aid provisions payments to employable persons will diminish their incentive to work cannot be ignored. In addition, income subsidies may not be used for the intended purpose of providing basic sustenance. Finally, semantics plays a significant role. The public may agree to pay allowances to poor people as they undergo training, but may be unwilling to support relief for the unemployed.

Included among the existing cash income maintenance programs are Old Age, Survivors, and Disability Insurance (OASDI), unemployment insurance, public assistance, veterans' pensions, and workers' compensation. Because public sentiment against income payments to employable persons apparently remains strong, these programs are aimed for the most part at persons outside of the work force or those who have been forced out of jobs. However, more comprehensive programs—such as guaranteed income, negative income tax, or family allowance—have been proposed to distribute income subsidies on the basis of need rather than labor force status.

Another group of programs provides goods and services directly to the needy, as a supplement to their cash income. Whatever the relative conceptual preferences between helping the poor with cash or in-kind income, political realities frequently dictate the latter. Public attention usually must be focused on a specific problem in order to mobilize society's resources. For example, increased food appropriations were forthcoming only after a highly publicized investigation of hunger in the late 1960s in the United States, and the resulting program was tailored to meet this specific problem. The program was expanded further in the mid-1970s as a response to high unemployment. It would have been infinitely more difficult to gain additional support for direct cash payments to the poor, which might or might not have been used to purchase a better diet.

Not only is in-kind aid more palatable politically, but it is argued that the government is often a better judge of needs and priorities than the individual. Moreover, in some instances the necessary goods are simply not available in the market and direct provision is more effective. For example, the construction of low-cost housing is not profitable and cannot be provided to the poor without direct government action, particularly where racial discrimination is involved. To grant housing subsidies to the poor without increasing the supply of housing would simply raise rents on existing units. In a similar manner, the government, in some cases, can provide a wide variety of goods and services more efficiently than the private sector because of the economies of large-scale enterprise.

Other services are provided directly by the government, not so much to make life easier for today's poor as to give their children a better chance to avoid poverty. Helping families to have no more children than they want is one of the most effective ways of eliminating poverty. It is also important to provide proper care for mother and child, so that the young will be healthy. The federal government also supports compensatory education programs for children of the poor from preschool to college.

Finally, programs aimed at restructuring institutions and improving the ability of the poor to work with these institutions are intended to eliminate the immediate causes of poverty rather than merely to mitigate its symptoms. For the most part, such programs are directed toward the employable poor, opening opportunities for them to free themselves from poverty. They tend to concentrate on economic institutions, although increasing recognition has been given to the fact that control over noneconomic institutions is often a prerequisite to economic opportunity.

These efforts can be divided into three groups: first, programs that seek to improve the individual's ability to compete in the labor market through training, placement, rehabilitation, and incentives to private employers to hire the disadvantaged; second, programs that attempt to restructure the labor market through minimum wage, public employment, and antidiscrimination efforts; third, programs designed to help redevelop depressed urban and rural areas—including Indian reservations—in order to bring employment opportunities to geographic "pockets of poverty."

In the end, of course, the several programs complement each other. Not only must we assuage today's poverty through cash and in-kind aid, but we must prevent it in the future by better preparing society's youth to fulfill their potential and by giving the poor a better chance in the job market. But it is not always easy to isolate the impact of these programs upon beneficiaries. Birth control and maternal care may be designed primarily to give the young a better start in life, but they also leave the mother in better condition to contribute to her own support. Similarly, the differentiation between cash support and "rehabilitative" programs is often blurred in reality. It is generally recognized, for example, that stipends must be paid to the poor if they are to undertake an effective training course.

Despite the rhetoric favoring cash assistance over in-kind aid, the trend in recent years has been in favor of the latter. In the 1970s, federal in-kind outlays have continued to expand and now exceed the traditional federally aided and locally administered cash assistance programs. In 1980 federal outlays per poor person were estimated at about $2,750, but only 39 percent was in cash. Fifteen years earlier, the annual assistance per poor person amounted to $770 (in 1979 dollars) and 81 percent was in cash.

Work and Welfare

Prevailing societal values often dictate that assistance programs be differentiated on the basis of the labor force status of recipients. Thus, programs aimed at the working poor have been distinguished from those designed to help people outside the labor force. The inherent difficulties of categorizing the poor according to labor force status are obvious, and official government definitions of the labor force offer only limited help. What is needed is a measure that would link employment and income and not just statistics that classify persons as employed, unemployed, or not in the labor force, without regard to their income.

15

Many poor people move in and out of the labor force depending upon overall economic conditions and personal circumstances. Also, with a growing system of income transfers, the decision to work or remain outside the labor force can be complex. Efforts to provide minimal adequate income for the nonworking poor, restrictive eligibility for the working poor, and benefit reductions due to any earnings have made welfare more attractive than work for many low-skilled, low-waged workers and has created an unexpected financial burden on the taxpayer.

It is also difficult to decide a priori which individuals should be provided basic income through work (wages) and which should be provided support through public assistance. For example, should a female head of family with minor dependents and no regular income be required to work for support or should the state assume the obligation of making direct contributions to her family's sustenance? Experts disagree over whether society would be better served by providing work for the mother—assuming jobs are available—or by providing sufficient income to allow the mother to devote full time to raising her children. As the number of working women with young children increases, the latter alternative becomes harder to defend. However, providing adequate employment for needy low-skilled family heads, particularly when provisions for child care are a necessary prerequisite, can be a costly proposition.

There is an increasing awareness that society may be best served by supplementing the income of the working poor and, conversely, by encouraging relief recipients to work without losing all or at least part of their public assistance. Because of this, the differentiation between programs for the working poor and those for persons outside the labor market is becoming less important in developing further aid programs. The food stamp program, which became a major aid program during the 1970s, operates very much like a negative income tax, and there seems to be increasing acceptance of the advisability of efforts that do not attempt to make distinctions based on labor force status.

Delivery of Services

Another problem in choosing antipoverty strategies is the administrative structure for the delivery of these services. Prior to the Great Society federal social programs were few and their budgets correspondingly slim. The federal government matched funds for public assistance and vocational education programs, but administration of these was largely left up to the states—even when the government supplied all of the funds, as it did in the case of employment services. One of the tenets of the Great Society, however, was to fund public and private local sponsors to implement national priorities, frequently bypassing involvement by elected state and local officials. It was assumed that federal expertise would be more efficiently applied to running the emerging new efforts aimed at combating poverty.

By the end of the 1960s, a reaction was building against the presumed unwieldiness of this apparatus. Grant-in-aid programs had proliferated and funds flowed from a variety of federal spigots. The result was often an uncoordinated tangle of programs in each locality, under the auspices of a maze of funding arrangements and operating guidelines.

To improve the delivery of services locally, proposals have been made for decentralization and decategorization of federal social programs. Both of these terms are generic and connote a philosophy rather than a specific method. "Decentralization" generally refers to a decline in the federal role in administering programs, and a concomitant increase in state and local authority. "Decategorization" refers to a reduction in the earmarking of funds for specific purposes by Congress, in order to give states and localities broader choice of spending priorities. Just as each governmental unit faces unique problems, the argument goes, so should it have the flexibility in committing resources and administering programs to meet these needs.

Congress enacted the first "revenue sharing" in 1972, by distributing to state and local governments about $6 billion a year, which could be used for a wide variety of purposes. But it is unrealistic to expect Congress to abdicate all responsibility for overseeing the funds that it raises, as would be required by complete decategorization and decentralization. In overhauling the numerous categorical employment and training efforts Congress rejected, in 1973, the administration's proposed revenue-sharing approach in favor of a federal-state-local partnership. The debate concerning the appropriate degree of federal control over its grants, the need to retain national programs, and the ability of local officials to administer the programs remains unresolved.

While Congress invariably pays lip service to local control, it continues to provide for categorical efforts that preclude genuine local control.

THE SCALE OF ANTIPOVERTY EFFORTS

The various programs for the poor involve a substantial aggregate cost even though exact measurement is not possible because many programs serve the nonpoor as well as the poor. Federal expenditures to help the poor were estimated to amount to close to $68 billion in 1980 (table 2). State and local expenditures might raise total governmental outlays by another 25 percent with private philanthropic efforts adding several billion dollars more if the value of volunteer charitable work is included. While these are rough estimates, it is fair to say that in 1980 the total price tag of programs in aid of the poor amounted to about $85 billion.

This estimate includes payments made to poor people who participated in programs available to all, and not just the resources

Table 2. Federal aid to the poor, 1964, 1970, 1974, and 1980

Program	1964	Fiscal (billions) 1970	1974	1980
Total	*$7.7*	*$17.9*	*$27.0*	*$67.5*
Cash	6.2	8.8	11.9	26.5
OASDI and railroad retirement	3.8	5.2	6.3	13.4
Public assistance	1.3	2.2	3.8	6.7
Veterans' pensions and compensation	0.8	1.0	1.0	1.7
Unemployment benefits	0.3	0.2	0.6	1.5
Other	[1]	0.1	0.2	3.2
Employment and training	0.2	1.5	2.0	6.7
Community and economic development	[1]	0.6	0.8	1.4
Education	0.1	1.4	1.8	4.3
Health	0.7	4.0	6.2	16.6
Housing	0.1	0.3	0.8	2.4
Household energy	—	—	—	1.1
Food	0.2	0.8	2.4	7.4
Child care and other social services	0.2	0.5	1.1	1.1

Source: U.S. Department of Commerce, *Statistical Abstract of the United States; 1975* (Washington: Government Printing Office, 1975), p. 405, and author's estimates for 1980, based on earlier estimates by Gordon Fisher.
Note: Details may not add to totals because of rounding.
[1]Less than $50 million

allocated on the basis of need. For example, the inclusion of Old Age, Survivors, Disability, and Health Insurance (OASDHI) as part of total welfare costs may be questioned by some because the program's eligibility test is based on prior contributions rather than personal need. But whatever the goals or criteria, all the programs included in this survey provide needed assistance to the poor, raising some out of poverty and reducing its severity for many others.

Crude as these estimates may be, they indicate a sustained effort to combat poverty, even if the resources allocated for the goal are not adequate to eradicate deprivation. The resources that the federal government has allocated in aid of the poor since the Great Society proclaimed the goal of eliminating poverty have grown consistently as a share of the federal budget as well as total disposable income available to the American people. Federal antipoverty funds have been rising as a percentage of:

	Total federal outlays	Total disposable income
1964	6.5	1.8
1970	9.1	2.6
1980	12.0	4.1 (1979)

Adjusted for inflation, the rise of the federal contribution for the poor has been equally impressive. By 1979, real outlays had risen 275 percent above the 1964 level of federal expenditures on the poor. More than two-thirds of this increase came about during the 1970s. These boosts in total outlays occurred while the number of poor was declining. On a per capita basis the real federal contribution for poor persons quadrupled.

No matter how much money and other resources American society contributes to its poor citizens, it is not possible to judge the adequacy of these contributions because no generally accepted criteria exist to suggest what percentage of the gross national product, or even of governmental expenditures, should be allocated to the poor. Nor are international comparisons of much help since needs and programs differ widely among countries. In the last analysis, the level of expenditures probably depends upon the public tolerance of deprivation in light of the general standard of living. The question is whether the rapid reduction of poverty can be made a primary and pressing

19

national goal. The experience of the 1970s offers little hope that poverty will be eliminated in the United States in the near future. However, major strides have been made in that direction. Poverty as defined by government statistics has been sharply reduced and, as was pointed out, the actual progress has been far greater than the official government data indicate because the official poverty count fails to take account of in-kind assistance which has expanded much more rapidly than cash assistance. Even if the media do not publicize the continued expansion of aid to the poor and political leaders in the 1970s have failed to take credit for the major accomplishments, the fact is that the price tag of programs in aid of the poor has grown.

Several decades ago, an authoritative foreign observer of the American scene, Nobel Prize winner Gunnar Myrdal, observed, "In almost all respects . . . American economic and social policies show a perverse tendency to favor groups that are above the level of the most needy." This comment may have had some validity in the past but it clearly does not reflect the transformation that occurred in American society since the Great Society.

ADDITIONAL READINGS

Browning, Edgar K. *Redistribution and the Welfare System.* Washington, D.C.: Government Printing Office, 1977.

Schiller, Bradley R. *The Economics of Poverty and Discrimination.* Englewood Clifs, N.J.: Prentice-Hall, 1980.

U.S. Congressional Budget Office. *Poverty Status of Families under Alternative Definitions of Income.* Washington, D.C.: Government Printing Office, 1977.

Poverty and Human Resources offers a complete quarterly review of the literature on poverty. Detailed data on poverty are presented annually in *Characteristics of the Low-Income Population* and *Money Income and Poverty Status of Families and Persons in the United States,* Current Population Reports, Series P–60, by the U.S. Bureau of the Census.

DISCUSSION QUESTIONS

1. Who are the poor in the United States and why are they poor?
2. How accurate are the Current Population Survey poverty estimates? What are the major shortcomings of these measurements?

3. Given the increase in employment and welfare outlays during the 1970s, why has there been no reduction in the number of poor persons during the decade?

4. Compare the pros and cons of counting the number of poor based on an arbitrary income level as contrasted with a poverty threshold based on a predetermined proportion of median individual or family income.

5. Do you believe that poverty would disappear within the next generation if 3 percent annual average growth in productivity is resumed?

6. "Inequality of family income is an inevitable characteristic of our economy." Discuss.

2

Cash Support Programs

You shall open wide your hand to your brother, to the needy, and to the poor.

—Deuteronomy 15:11

In 1980 about one of every three Americans received assistance from public programs. The total cost was over $300 billion, four-fifths of which was paid in cash. The poor are much more likely to receive cash transfer payments than are the nonpoor (figure 4). And many of the nonpoor would have been poor without these transfers. An estimated 10.7 million families were kept out of poverty in 1976 by cash transfers.

The Social Security Act, the product of more than four decades of evolution since its enactment in 1935, is the most significant income maintenance program for both the poor and the nonpoor. Programs contained in this act accounted for eight-tenths of the income support for the poor and for about two-thirds of the payments to the nonpoor. Two groups of programs established by the act were: (1) social insurance programs—including Old Age, Survivors, and Disability Insurance and unemployment insurance—both of which distribute payments on the basis of prior earnings and prior tax contributions; and (2) public assistance programs—for the elderly, the blind, the disabled, and families with dependent children—which provide income support on the basis of need alone (figure 5).

Figure 4 Sources of income, poor and all families, 1978

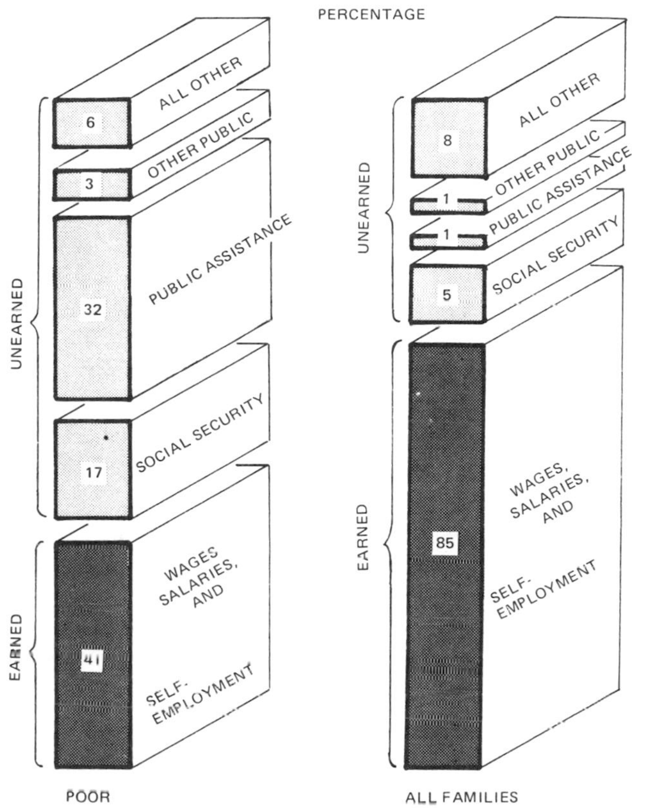

PERCENTAGE

SOURCE: U.S. Bureau of the Census

OASDI

Old Age, Survivors, and Disability Insurance (OASDI) distributes more income to the poor than any other government transfer program. One poor family in four receives these benefits. In addition, these income supports have prevented many households from falling into poverty. However, eligibility and benefit levels are determined *not* by recipients' current income but by their past contributions.

23

Figure 5 Government outlays for income security cash payments

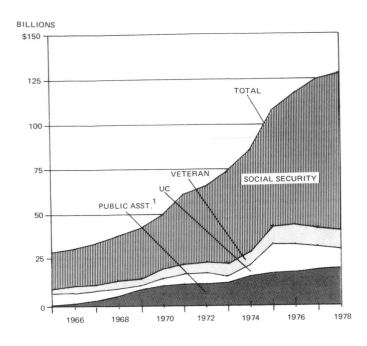

SOURCE: *The U.S. Budget in Brief, Fiscal Year 1981.*

The social security system is vast. Old Age, Survivors, and Disability Insurance expenditures alone totaled $115 billion in 1980 (excluding $34 billion paid for hospital and medical insurance). Some 35 million persons—one American in seven—received regular cash payments. Coverage is extensive: nine of every ten people in paid employment or self-employment are covered; of those who reached age 65 in 1978, only 6 percent were not eligible for some benefits; 95 percent of all children and their mothers would receive benefits if the father were to die.

Both the benefits and the burden of OASDI have fallen disproportionately on the bottom of the income spectrum. Until the late 1970s only earnings below the median were taxed. To boost social security

24

revenue Congress raised the taxable earnings to cover the total earnings of most workers. In 1980 the program was financed by a 12.3 percent tax (including 2 percent for health insurance) on annual earnings up to $25,900 shared equally by an employee and the payrolls and to be extended to cover the total earnings of the bulk of wage and salary earners. To the extent that the employer's contributions are part of the worker's defined earnings, the total tax amounts to about one dollar of every eight of the employee's compensation. Furthermore, there are no exemptions for the lowest-paid workers or for those with large families, therefore making the tax a relatively heavier burden on large poor families.

On the other hand, lower-income workers benefit disproportionately. A fully covered single individual retiring at age 65 with maximum average monthly insured earnings of $784 would have received monthly benefits equal to 73 percent of that amount; a retiree with earnings of $400 would have received 92 percent in benefits; and a retiree with $100 in monthly earnings would have received 172 percent. The highest-paid worker would have paid about seven times as much in tax contributions but would have received benefits only three times as great.

The extent to which OASDI should redistribute income is widely debated but it now does so in two ways. It transfers money from the higher-paid retiree to the lower-paid retiree by granting relatively more generous benefits to the latter. It also transfers money from the generation now working to the retired generation. OASDI is said to be an "insurance" system but, unlike a commercial insurance company, which invests premiums to pay for future claims, the federal government collects only enough in taxes to finance current expenditures and keeps in the "trust fund" an amount equal to only one year's benefits.

Individuals must be insured in order to receive benefits. Persons with 40 quarters of coverage are permanently insured. The basic benefit payable to a retired or disabled worker is related to the worker's age and to the level of covered earnings. Dependents and survivors can receive set proportions of this benefit, subject to a family maximum. Two exceptions are: a special benefit of $92 per month for persons who reached age 72 before 1968 and who had no covered work, and a special benefit of up to $253 for workers with prolonged years of covered employment at low wages.

Social security benefits are not means tested, but they can be reduced if the recipient continues to work. For beneficiaries aged 65 to 71, payments are reduced 50 cents for each dollar of earnings above $5,000. "Earnings" are considered income from labor, but not income from rents, royalties, or dividends. According to this, a beneficiary aged 65 to 71 loses one dollar of every two above $5,000 in wages or salaries but income from interest, dividends, or gains made in the stock market do not affect social security benefits. Starting in 1982, beneficiaries 70 years of age and older will not be subject to a benefit reduction due to earnings.

Although OASDI has continued to expand, several flaws remain in coverage and benefits. Some 7 percent of those between 65 and 72 years of age are not eligible for benefits. There remains the inequity that a wife's earnings effect a higher family retirement income only if they would result in total family benefits that are 50 percent larger than the husband's benefits. Finally, despite several recent increases, benefits remain inadequate to raise all recipients above the poverty threshold. In 1979 about 7 percent of cash beneficiaries aged 65 and over also received means-tested welfare supplemental security payments. The average monthly benefit of $339 in July 1980 left the retired worker just barely escaping poverty, but the average retired couple received benefits 22 percent above the poverty level (figure 6). An individual with the minimum benefit would receive $139 per month, less than half the poverty level. To protect the income of retired workers from inflation, the law provides that benefits be adjusted when the cost of living rises by at least 3 percent in one year. While social security is the single most important program for reducing poverty, it is not the most cost-effective approach, even for the aged.

Old age insurance provides income to a steadily rising portion of the aged population—up to 94 percent in 1980. Workers receive their full entitlement at age 65, but they can claim benefits earlier with a corresponding permanent decrease in the amount. At age 62, the earliest age to retire, the reduction is 20 percent. Because many of those who choose lower benefits were forced into early retirement by job loss or disability, and because they typically earned less than workers who wait until age 65, the permanent reduction in benefits is

Figure 6 Social Security benefits, July 1980[1]

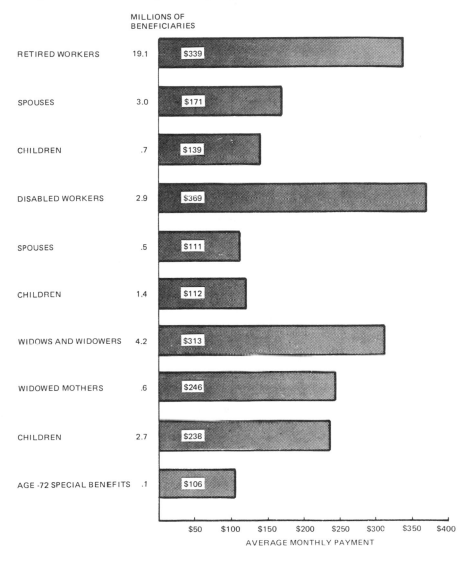

SOURCE: U.S. Department of Health and Human Services
 [1]Preliminary estimates

27

harsh. On the other hand, workers can increase their benefits by 1 percent for each year beyond 65 they postpone retirement.

Survivors insurance is payable to an insured worker's surviving children under 18 years of age (under 22 if they attend school), to the parents of these children, to dependent parents, and to dependent widows or widowers. Finally, disability insurance provides for severely disabled adults (aged 18 to 64) who are not able to engage in substantial gainful employment. To be eligible for insurance payments, they must have worked at least 20 to 40 quarters prior to disability, or, in the case of workers disabled before age 24, they must have worked half of the quarters (but not fewer than six) since turning 21. Disability benefits are paid after a waiting period of five months, and medical proof of disability is required, along with a determination that the disability rules out gainful employment. About one-fourth of the estimated 8 million severely disabled adults receive disability insurance.

PUBLIC ASSISTANCE

In addition to distributing benefits under OASDI to insured workers or their survivors, the Social Security Act provides Aid to Families with Dependent Children (AFDC) and assistance to the aged, blind, and disabled through the Supplemental Security Income (SSI) program. Persons not eligible under one of these federally aided programs may receive state-funded and locally funded general assistance. Of these programs, AFDC is by far the largest, constituting nearly seven-tenths of the 15.2 million recipients in mid-1979 and well over half of the nearly $19 billion in 1979 expenditures. AFDC is identified with "welfare" because it accounted for most of the increase in means-tested income support after World War II (figure 7).

SSI generally offers substantially higher benefits than AFDC and general assistance. Although public assistance lifts many persons out of poverty, over half of the families reporting public assistance income in 1978 were poor despite this aid.

Aid to Families with Dependent Children

By far the largest, costliest, and most controversial public assistance program is Aid to Families with Dependent Children. In mid-1979

Figure 7 AFDC accounted for most of the welfare increase after World War II

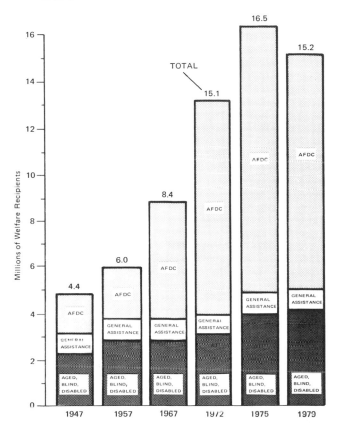

SOURCE: U.S. Department of Health and Human Services

there were over 10 million recipients, including 7.2 million children, or more than one child in every eleven. Benefits paid during that year totaled about $11 billion.

Though the federal government contributes more than half of the total cost of AFDC, it delegates administration of the program to the states, within broad federal guidelines. The federal government pays about five-ninths of AFDC costs, state governments pay one-third, and local governments pay one-ninth. Most important, the states determine eligibility standards and the level of benefits. The grant paid to the recipient is based on need standards determined by each state, and may vary widely from state to state. The standard nominally reflects the cost of rent, utilities, food, clothing, and other basic expenses. In many states, however, there is little correlation between actual living costs and the established need standards. The monthly cost of basic needs calculated by the states for a family of four on AFCD in 1978 ranged from $187 to $566; the median was $334. But many states fail to pay even these low standards under AFDC. Varying rules determine the difference between need and public assistance payments. Only twenty-two states pay up to the full amount under AFDC. Others set maximum benefits that are below standard needs or pay only a fixed percentage of the standard. In nine states the maximum amount paid to a family with no income is less than two-thirds of the minimum standards. Considering the stinginess of "standard need" definitions, the failure to make up this deficit leaves most public assistance recipients in deprivation. The average state maximum payment to AFDC families was $386. States with relatively low per capita income tend to pay lower benefits. In 1978 no state paid high enough benefits to keep an AFDC family out of poverty if it had no other income or in-kind assistance. Map 1 shows the range of average benefit payments and the parsimoniousness of some states.

AFDC growth since World War II has been substantial—doubling each decade between 1947 and 1967 and again between 1967 and 1972, when the expansion virtually ceased (except for a mild increase during the recession in the mid-1970s) as the bulk of female-headed poor families qualified for assistance. That AFDC rose so rapidly during the 1960s was especially remarkable since the poverty population declined during that decade. The reasons for the expansion of AFDC are many and complex. Not only did more people become eligible, but the benefits were also increased and the stigma attendant to welfare was reduced.

There was considerable population growth in the quarter century after World War II, especially among children. But perhaps more important were changes in family structure resulting in an increasing number of households headed by women who are potential AFDC

Map 2. Average Monthly AFDC Payments Per Person, June 1979

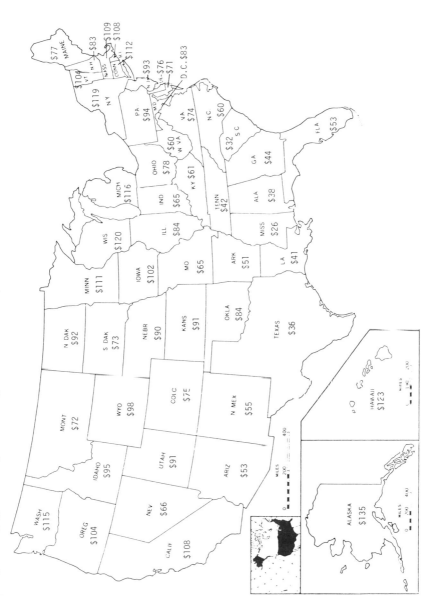

MAINE $77
VT $104
N.H. $83
MASS $109
R.I. $108
CONN $112
N.Y. $119
N J $93
DEL $76
MD $71
D.C. $83
PA $94
VA $74
N.C. $60
W VA $60
OHIO $78
KY $61
S.C. $32
GA $44
FLA $53
MICH $116
IND $65
TENN $42
ALA $38
WIS $120
ILL $84
MISS $26
IOWA $102
MO $65
ARK $51
LA $41
MINN $111
NEBR $90
KANS $91
OKLA $84
N DAK $92
S DAK $73
TEXAS $36
MONT $72
WYO $98
COLO $75
N MEX $55
IDAHO $95
UTAH $91
ARIZ $53
WASH $115
OREG $104
NEV $66
CALIF $108
HAWAII $123
ALASKA $135

MILES
0   200   400

MILES
0   100   200

MILES
0   200   400

recipients. Not only did the rate of divorce increase 50 percent during the 1960s, but the number of children involved per divorce decree also increased. Although data are imprecise for desertions and separations without court decree—the "poor man's divorce"—these, too, became more numerous. Out-of-wedlock births multiplied from one in twenty to one in ten. But cause and effect cannot readily be disentangled. AFDC may be viewed as a response to economic and social pressures resulting from the rise of the single-parent family, but the program itself may induce families to modify their behavior in order to qualify for benefits. AFDC may encourage the very phenomenon to which it is a response by inducing an unemployed man either to desert his family to make his dependents eligible for assistance or to fail to marry the mother. However, charges that mothers on welfare have additional children in order to qualify for higher payments remain unsubstantiated and many AFDC mothers seek and practice birth control when it is made available. The average AFDC family has 2.9 persons, and over four-fifths of the families have three or fewer children.

Supreme Court decisions and federal legislation have added to the welfare population by extending coverage to groups not previously eligible. In 1961 Congress allowed states to grant assistance to families that were dependent because of the unemployment of an employable parent. This "unemployed parent" component, now available in 27 states, is restricted by federal regulations to those working fewer than 100 hours per month, no matter how meager their earnings. Most important was that 1967 provision to disregard $30 per month plus work expenses and one-third of additional earnings. In 1968 the court struck down the "man in the house" rule, which held a man living in an AFDC house responsible for the children's support even if he was not legally liable. The following year the Supreme Court invalidated residency requirements for public assistance. Later, states were permitted to grant aid to children after age 18 who were attending school. Income disregards—whereby states ignore certain earnings in computing eligibility and payments—have permitted many families who would otherwise have been disqualified to remain on the rolls.

While these developments increased the number of persons eligible for assistance, neighborhood legal services agencies, the welfare rights organizations, and other groups publicized the availability of, and eligibility requirements for, AFDC benefits. Improvements in the administration of assistance attracted more applicants as the wait between application and approval was shortened.

Finally, a basic condition for growth was the broader attractiveness of AFDC relative to other sources of income. As the federal government assumed a larger share of the burden, states became less reluctant to qualify individuals for aid and to provide more adequate benefits. Between 1947 and 1962 average AFDC payments and spendable average weekly earnings of all private employees rose equally; but between 1963 and 1978 the AFDC payment increased 162 percent while earnings rose only 130 percent, 45 percent of which was a reflection of the rise in prices over this period. And significant increases in the use of food stamps and medical care—not reflected in the cash payments—tilted the balance even more in favor of welfare. (These in-kind income supplements are discussed in chapter 4.) Although working may still provide more income than public assistance alone to many families on welfare, combining these two sources may be preferable to either. In addition to the higher measurable benefits of welfare, the stigma of "being on relief" probably declined. Government income support became much more widely distributed, reaching almost one-third of the population by 1980. AFDC recipients alone constitute more than one-tenth of the populations of New York City, Philadelphia, Baltimore, Boston, St. Louis, New Orleans, Detroit, and the District of Columbia.

These forces contributed to the rapid expansion of AFDC in the 1960s. But public reaction against welfare, state cutbacks in benefits, and the imposition of new work requirements on recipients arrested the growth in the rolls since 1972. There was little growth through 1980 except for a slight increase resulting from the high level of unemployment during the mid-1970s. AFDC rolls peaked in 1975 and actually declined in the latter half of the decade. Although administration officials attributed this leveling off to better management, others believe that most eligible persons had already joined the aid rolls.

AFDC recipients are disadvantaged in many ways, but they are not a class unto themselves. Fathers are present in only one AFDC home in nine, and over half of these men are disabled. Nearly half of AFDC families are nonwhite. AFDC mothers have substantially lower educational attainment than other women of the same age level: about twice as many had completed eight or fewer years of school. Their work experience also has serious limitations. Nearly one-fourth have never been employed, and of those who have worked, one-fourth are in private household and other unskilled employment, which generally provide meager earnings. The average number of children per family was 2.3, but nearly one-third of the families included at least one child born out of wedlock.

The outlook for AFDC families is not completely bleak. As their numbers increased, AFDC recipients' characteristics and aspirations became increasingly similar to the rest of the population's. Close to one-third of adult recipients is either working or looking for work, and this proportion is slowly rising. Their educational attainment, although still relatively low, is also rising. More have some paid work experience. Most significantly, studies have shown that AFDC recipients are no less eager to work than the rest of the population. In fact, since 1969 they have had a general incentive to supplement their income through earnings because the law provided that work expenses and the first $30 of earnings, plus one-third of additional earnings, could be disregarded in computing welfare benefits. Before 1969, many states had reduced benefits dollar-for-dollar as earnings increased; this "100 percent tax" certainly stifled incentives to seek work and to improve family income.

Although the "$30 and ⅓" incentive is part of federal law, the total amount of earnings that are ignored (or disregarded) in computing the assistance check varies from state to state. Some jurisdictions are very liberal in computing work expenses, while others are strict. Because of the spread in payment levels, the hourly earnings level required to remove a family of four from AFDC is more than $3.50 in many states. There are not many AFDC mothers who could qualify for such jobs—assuming they are available—and continue working full time, year-round, and thus work their way off the welfare rolls.

Although the employability of many AFDC mothers is limited, it has become more acceptable for a female family head to work and child care facilities are expanding. Thus it is no accident that for more and more recipients, work and welfare go together. Just as poverty is often transitory, most families do not languish forever on welfare. In recent years, as many as three-tenths of new cases left the public assistance rolls within a year and three-fourths closed within three years. In 1977 one AFDC family in three had not been on the rolls in 1976.

There can also be an inequity between families on welfare and those not on the rolls, because the work incentive applies only to those who are already receiving assistance. Thus, in a state whose eligibility level is $340 per month, a women earning $360 would not qualify. But if her neighbor had already qualified for aid and then took a job paying $360 per month, the neighbor would keep not only all the earnings but at least $140 of her assistance check [$30 + ⅓ ($360 − $30)], for a total income of $500, and this amount does take into consideration work-connected expenses. Indeed, in some states the employed AFDC mother may retain the bulk of her welfare payments. This incentive, paradoxically, may encourage some working poor family heads to quit their jobs, seek welfare, and then resume working. Combining work and welfare can be more preferable to drawing on either source alone.

The increasing tendency is to treat work and welfare as complements; three-fifths of the families who remained poor in 1978 had earned income and three-fourths received some welfare assistance. Welfare alone was rarely adequate to raise a family above poverty, and only two-fifths of all poor families depended exclusively on welfare.

Supplemental Security Income

For nearly four decades assistance programs for the aged, blind, and disabled operated similarly to AFDC. Although the federal government contributed a share of the cost, state and local governments largely determined eligibility and benefit levels and administered the programs. Benefits were more generous than under AFDC, but they too varied widely.

Social Security amendments passed in 1972 thoroughly revamped this system. As of 1980 the federal government guaranteed the aged, blind, and disabled a monthly income of $208 for an individual and $312 for a couple under the Supplemental Security Income (SSI) program. This represented an increase in benefits paid by nearly half the states. Even so, the guarantee equaled only about 73 percent of the poverty level for individuals and 83 percent for couples. States can supplement the federal guarantee, but without federal contributions.

The law also provided that $20 per month of social security payments or other income, plus $65 of earned income and half of additional earnings, be disregarded in computing eligibility. It is ironic that the aged, blind, and disabled—whose ability to work is probably limited—have much more attractive incentives than do recipients of AFDC, many of whom can and should be encouraged to work. One explanation of the congressional generosity is the anticipation that in the case of these groups the liberal incentives carried a very low price tag.

The law substituted federal eligibility standards to the aged, blind, and disabled. The demeaning "declarations of indebtedness" required by many states to ensure that only the most destitute received benefits were eliminated. A lien on a welfare recipient's property netted little for the state but took a heavy toll in self-respect. The federal law, nonetheless, retained stringent standards. Aside from a home, an automobile, property for self-support, and life insurance policies worth less than $1,500, the assets of aged, blind, or disabled public assistance recipients could not exceed $1,500 for an individual or $2,250 for a couple. The intent of the law was to protect the taxpayer from the claims of those not in need, without debasing the recipient.

Congress expected these changes to channel more income to the aged, blind, and disabled. Program costs increased from $3.2 billion in fiscal 1972 (under the three separate programs) to an estimated $7.8 billion in 1980, including $1.4 billion in benefits paid by 27 states. The average monthly number of recipients rose from 3.1 million in fiscal 1972, the year prior to the enactment of SSI, to 4.2 million by the end of 1979.

The transition from local to federal administration of SSI was accompanied by the traditional problems that characterized locally administered welfare programs—high administrative costs and eligibility conflicts. Many of the expected benefits of federalization were slow to be realized.

Experience under the previous, separate programs showed that the number of aged recipients had declined by more than one-quarter since its peak in 1950. Similarly, the number of blind recipients had also declined. Aid to the disabled, however, began only in 1951 and the number of recipients had increased steadily to the 2.2 million mark by 1979. The sharp decline in the first category was generally attributed to the spread of the social security system. As the number of aged welfare recipients dropped from 2.8 million in 1950 to 1.9 million in mid-1979, the number of OASDI recipients aged 65 and over grew from 2.6 million to 22.6 million. And the proportion of old age assistance recipients who also received OASDI climbed steadily to 70 percent.

Aged, blind, and disabled recipients of aid are likely to be old, white, and female:

	Median age	Proportion white	Proportion female
Aged	76	65	72
Blind	56	64	56
Disabled	52	65	60

These rolls were fairly stable: the mean duration on assistance was over five years for the aged and six years for the blind; that it was under three years for the disabled is partly due to the rapid growth of this program. The aged were typically alone and without other support. Only one-fifth were living with their spouses, though close to nine of every ten maintained their own households. Only 13 percent had unearned income other than from federal programs at an average of $58 a month. Their capacity for self-support was meager, not at all surprising among a population with an average age of 76 and one of every three above age 80. Only 2 percent of recipients were working in late 1978. Of the 24 million persons 65 years of age and over in 1978, nearly one in seven, or 3.3 million, was poor. The number of aged poor had declined by over 1.5 million during the preceding decade largely as a result of higher welfare benefits, including social security, supplementary security income, and veterans' benefits.

More than six of every seven blind persons on public assistance lived in their own households. One of every seven was under 18 years of age. Remarkably, 7 percent were working full or part time, but a significant proportion had never worked. In addition to lack of vision, many had one or more chronic health problems.

The disabled were afflicted by a variety of impediments, both mental and physical. Over four-fifths of adult recipients maintain their own households. The proportion of recipients who were confined has

37

dropped significantly in recent years. Only a relatively small proportion of disabled recipients also receive vocational rehabilitation.

The aged, blind, and disabled are considered less capable of self-support and less responsible for their dependency than AFDC recipients, and hence are deemed more "deserving" of aid. This public judgment is clearly reflected in notably higher benefits and more humane administration.

General Assistance

For the needy who do not qualify for federally supported aid, most states provide varying coverage and benefits through general assistance. Some provide cash payments; others limit assistance to medical care, hospitalization, or burial. In mid-1979 there were a total of 760,000 persons on general assistance rolls in 42 states. The monthly outlay per recipient amounted to $130, ranging from a low of $13 in Mississippi to $160 in New York. Three states—Illinois, New York, and Pennsylvania—accounted for two-thirds of the caseload and expenditures. Clearly, most states made very meager provisions for persons who do not qualify for federally supported income programs. In Pennsylvania there was 1 general assistance beneficiary for every 4 recipients of AFDC; in California, 1 for every 35; and in Alabama, 1 for every 4,000.

General assistance cases are concentrated in large cities. The total number of general assistance recipients has fluctuated considerably over the years, typically rising during economic slumps. Because of rapid turnover, there may be twice as many recipients during a year than at any given time.

Veteran's Assistance

Income support on a preferential basis has long been available to a selected segment of the population—the 30 million veterans and their families who comprise over two-fifths of the total population. This type of income support predates even the Revolutionary War. Colonial laws mandated public support for men incapacitated in defense of the community. Although present programs do not provide enough support to permit all veterans and their dependents to escape poverty, they go a long way toward providing basic needs, particularly for older veterans and indigent survivors of deceased veterans.

Figure 8 Veterans income support, 1980 (total—$11.3 billion)

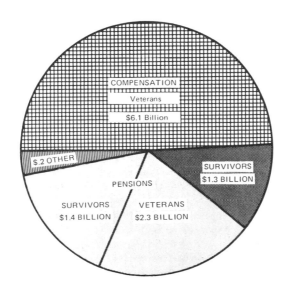

SOURCE: U.S. Veterans Administration

Two types of cash benefits, compensation and pensions, are provided. The cost to the federal government in 1980 was over $11.3 billion (figure 8). Compensation is paid to veterans (or their dependents) for an injury, disability, or death incurred while serving in the armed forces, and pensions are paid to war veterans (or their dependents) whose annual income is below a specified level and who are permanently and totally disabled. In practice the disability qualifications for a pension are relaxed as the veteran advances in age. The pension qualifications are more stringent for veterans below the age of 55, but veterans aged 65 and over may qualify on the basis of need. Altogether about one-fifth of total cash payments to veterans go to poor people.

Compensation

One of every thirteen veterans received compensation in 1980 for service-connected disability at a total budgeted cost to the government of $6.1 billion. Individual annual compensation averaged $2,692

39

ranging from $576 for a 10 percent disability to $10,668 for total disability. The payment to veterans with 30 percent or more disability is supplemented for dependents. Additional special compensation paid to veterans who suffered total blindness, deafness, or loss of limbs may boost the payment to $30,432 annually.

Congress periodically raises the level of compensation benefits to keep pace with rising living costs. Average annual compensation costs are likely to increase somewhat even in the absence of a rise in benefits because service-connected disabilities tend to become aggravated with advancing age. However, the higher mortality rate of injured persons diminishes the potential rise in benefits if these veterans were to live out their normal life span. Four of every ten World War II veterans who were receiving compensation in 1980 qualified for only minimum disability benefits (10 percent impairment), compared with almost one of every five World War I veterans. At the other extreme, 10 percent of World War I veterans who were receiving compensation were totally disabled, compared with 4.3 percent of World War II veterans. Because older veterans are more likely to suffer severe impairment, the average monthly compensation for World War I veterans was significantly higher than for World War II veterans—$254 as compared to $192 in 1979.

Data are not available on the income level of veterans receiving service-connected compensation. However, a 1971 study found that veterans receiving compensation had lower annual incomes than their nondisabled peers, and many of the disabled would have been counted among the poor had they not received compensation. This is particularly true of the nearly 478,000 (out of a total of 2.2 million) whose degree of impairment was 50 percent or more. Many of these disabled veterans were probably unable to hold full-time jobs.

A total of $1,322 million in survivors benefits was distributed in 1980 among 360,000 dependents of servicemen who died as the result of military service. Benefits are provided under dual programs; death compensation, in effect prior to 1957, is paid to over one-fifth of the cases, and dependency and indemnity compensation is received by four-fifths of the cases. Eligibility for the latter benefits is not means-tested with the exception since 1957 of qualifying dependent parents.

Death compensation pays a flat annual rate of $1,044 to a surviving spouse and $1,452 to a widow or widower with one dependent child. A dependent parent receives $900 annually and, unlike dependency and indemnity compensation for parents, payment is not means-tested or reduced in relation to other income.

Rates of dependency and indemnity compensation vary with the rank held by the deceased serviceman. Annual stipends range from $3,912 for a recruit's widow to $10,020 for a chief-of-staff's widow. The basic entitlement is increased $35 a month for each dependent child, and a widow who is housebound or in need of aid and attendants is entitled to an additional $89 a month. For dependents of veterans, compensation alone barely places widows of low-ranking servicemen above the poverty threshold; however, most widows with dependent children and those over 62 years are eligible for concurrent social security benefits. Parents are eligible for support if the income does not exceed $4,038 for a single parent or $5,430 for both parents. Maximum benefits of $1,956 and $2,616, respectively, are reduced in relation to other income.

Pensions

A total of 1.0 million war veterans received $2.3 billion in disability pensions in 1980, at an average of $2,351 for the year. These pensions are paid under three separate systems. For those on pension rolls prior to July 1960, an annual pension of $945 was payable to single veterans whose income was $3,884 or less in 1980. The income limitation for veterans with one dependent was $5,603. Under this plan the veteran's net worth and his wife's earnings were not considered in computing annual income.

In 1960 Congress added a sliding scale of benefits based on the beneficiary's level of income. Veterans or their survivors who qualified for pensions prior to enactment of the 1960 law could retain the old benefits or choose to qualify under the new system which provided in 1980 a maximum annual pension of $2,364 for a single veteran and $2,544 if he or she had a dependent. The sliding scale of benefits operating under the 1960 law reduces the pensions paid to relatively more affluent veterans by adjusting the annuity on the basis of the recipient's other income. This system also removes the possibility that veterans with higher earnings might receive pensions yielding them less total income than those with lower earnings. For example, a single veteran with an annual income of $1,000 is entitled to a $2,004 pension, giving a combined income of $3,004. A veteran with an annual income of $1,500 receives a pension of $1,596 for a combined income of $3,096.

To qualify for a pension under this sliding scale, a veteran without dependents must earn no more than $4,438 a year, and a veteran with one dependent, no more than $5,968. However, a married veteran may qualify for a pension even if the total annual family income is above the prescribed limit because the first $1,200 of the spouse's unearned income plus all earnings are excluded for the purpose of qualifying for this pension.

Congress restructured the entire pension system in 1979 to link pension to total family income and to provide cost-of-living adjustments concurrent with the increases in social security benefits. With these changes and with increased benefit levels, a third program of pension benefits came into use. Fundamentally, it is similar to the sliding scale benefit payment outlined above. Under this program, the benefit payment is equal to the difference between the veteran's income and the maximum allowable benefit payment using a broader interpretation of family countable income. With improved benefits, a single veteran with an annual income of $1,000 is entitled to $2,902 pension, giving a combined income of $3,902. A veteran with $1,500 of annual income would receive a pension of $2,402, giving the same combined income of $3,902 as received by the veteran with only $1,000 prebenefit income. However, a "grandfather" provision in the measure permitted veterans whose benefits would be lowered under the new formula to remain under the old system.

Over three-fourths of pensioned veterans are also eligible to receive OASDI benefits. VA data indicate that only one in four pensioned veterans had an annual income of less than $1,000, and these veterans were entitled to a minimum annual pension of about $2,004.

Dependents of deceased veterans may also qualify for pensions. Benefits are paid to the children until they reach age 18 or age 23 if they remain in school. A veteran's child is ineligible for a pension if the child's annual earned income exceeds $3,626 or if the estate is large enough to support the child.

Altogether, 1.2 million survivors received $1.8 billion in 1980, averaging $1,201 per family. Between 1965 and 1980 the number of widows of deceased World War II veterans who were receiving pensions more than tripled. If recent trends continue, the number of widows of World War II veterans qualifying for pensions will rise as the mortality rate of veterans increases and qualifying income levels are relaxed.

Since most veterans' widows with children also qualify for social security benefits, the combined potential income of veterans' survivors has significantly reduced the number of poor. Almost half of pensioned widows, however, still remained below the poverty threshold.

In contrast with the public assistance programs, veterans' benefits are administered with maximum consideration to the recipients' dignity and self-respect. Provided the veteran can prove eligibility, he or she has only to file a simple form in order to qualify. Thereafter the veteran is required to submit annually only the information needed by the Veterans Administration to keep the claim current and active. The annual data are filed on a simple form, supplied to the veteran or the dependent, which includes information about the veteran's assets, income, and dependents eligible to receive benefits. Once eligibility is established, the Veterans Administration makes only a cursory check on claims. Though the General Accounting Office has criticized these methods of certification, the Veterans Administration insists that the trust is justified, since spot checks made with the Internal Revenue Service in cases of questionable claims show that the incidence of false claims is small. Assistance to veterans and their surviving dependents is delivered with a maximum of respect for the recipient and a minimum of delay. The system is worthy of emulation by other public assistance programs in which onerous needs tests are made at the expense of services to the needy and at little savings to the taxpayer.

UNEMPLOYMENT INSURANCE

The objective of unemployment insurance (UI) is to provide essential aid to workers during periods of forced idleness. Unemployment insurance is not to be viewed as an antipoverty program, but as a protection earned by the worker against joblessness. Eligibility for assistance and the level of benefits are based on past earnings and work experience and not on need, so the poor are often excluded or receive inadequate benefits. The purpose of unemployment insurance is to cover nondeferrable expenditures, but without reducing the recipient's incentive to work.

Unemployment insurance was established along with the other social insurance programs under the Social Security Act of 1935. However, it was given a unique administrative structure. The law made employers in all states liable to a payroll tax; at 1980 levels the tax was 3.4 percent of the first $6,000 of an employee's annual earnings. Seventy-nine percent of the taxes are returned to the states for the operation of their own programs and the rest of the funds are earmarked for the administrative costs of the program and the federal-state extended benefit program. While state programs are subject to a few federal standards, such as the extent of coverage, the states determine the duration and amount of benefits, the eligibility of the covered worker, and the amount of the employer's contribution through a system that allows reduced tax burdens for employers who have a low unemployment experience. Therefore, it is to the employer's advantage to have state statutes that include as many barriers to qualification as possible. As a result, individual state programs vary widely even though the tax is universal. Three additional unemployment insurance programs are administered by the federal government for veterans, railroad workers, and federal government employees.

In order to establish eligibility for unemployment benefits, a worker in covered employment who finds himself out of work must meet the state's employment and earning tests, be available for work, and register with the local employment service office. Normally a weekly report of the individual's efforts to seek employment independently must be made to the employment service office.

States have additional eligibility rules that may exclude the poor from unemployment compensation. The covered worker typically must have been employed during two of the last five quarters, and most states require that earnings during the qualifying period be at least thirty times the weekly benefit amount, or a flat minimum sum ranging from $600 to $1,200 during the base period. The effect of minimum earning requirements is to force low-wage earners, who are most susceptible to unemployment, to work longer than high-wage earners in order to qualify for unemployment benefits. Also excluded are those unemployed who are just entering or reentering the labor force and those who either have been terminated for misconduct or have left their jobs voluntarily. These and other criteria disqualify more than half of all unemployed persons at any given time.

A related problem (and one that is more significant to the poor) concerns the relationship of unemployment benefits to those who leave the labor force to enroll in employment and training programs. The stipends paid to institutional training enrollees do not count toward unemployment insurance eligibility if the enrollee should have difficulty locating employment after leaving the program.

Weekly unemployment insurance benefits amounts vary widely among states. Most states compute benefits as a fraction of the worker's weekly or quarterly earnings, with maximums that are fixed amounts or fixed proportions of the state's average weekly wage; allowances are made for dependents in nine states. In 1980 maximum benefits for a claimant with dependents ranged from $74 per week in Indiana to $202 in Ohio. Since most states had maximums higher than $100, it is clear that benefits paid to the poorest recipients are limited more by previous low personal income than by the state maximums. The working poor would be helped more by raising the percentage of the claimant's income on which benefits are paid than by boosts in maximum payments.

The duration of benefits is often as crucial to the recipient as the average weekly payment. Until recently maximum duration of payments was normally 26 weeks. As a cushion against massive unemployment experienced during the 1970s, Congress extended benefits. The Extended Unemployment Compensation Act of 1970 provided that when the national seasonally adjusted insured unemployment rate exceeded 4.5 percent for three consecutive months, the duration of benefits in all states would automatically be extended by 13 weeks. Individuals states can extend benefits for a 13-week period if their covered unemployment rate is about 4 percent and is equal to 120 percent of the same period a year earlier. But this proved too short as the recession deepened and the long-term unemployed exhausted their eligibility. Accordingly, the duration of benefits was temporarily lengthened to 65 weeks in 1974. These measures provided a necessary back-up system during 1976 when an estimated 4.1 million individuals exhausted regular unemployment insurance and an additional 2.8 million exhausted the 13 weeks of eligibility.

These measures, no doubt, saved many from poverty. More comprehensive protection carried a substantial price tag with total costs for fiscal 1976 of $17 billion. The amount paid out in unemployment insurance decreased to $11 billion in 1979, nearly double the level paid before the recession in the mid-1970s.

More frequent and more prolonged unemployment among the poor is a significant cause of poverty. It is quite likely, then, that an increase in average benefits under unemployment insurance programs and the relaxation of eligibility based on earnings would reduce the number of poor. The potential of unemployment benefits as an antipoverty device is limited by the fact that it *is* an insurance program. During 1974, only an estimated 10 percent of unemployment benefits were paid to the poor. As long as the amount and duration of benefits are dependent on past work experience, those in the lowliest occupations with the highest incidence of poverty will be helped the least.

Workers covered under the Social Security Act, unemployment insurance, and the three separate federal unemployment compensation programs include over 88 percent of the work force. Many of the excluded workers are primarily state and local government employees and farm and domestic workers. The latter two groups are characterized by low income and intermittent employment. The incidence of poverty is also undoubtedly greater among these groups. High unemployment rates, averaging 8.5 percent in 1975, prompted Congress to pass several emergency provisions. Among them was a temporary measure to extend coverage to unemployed domestics, farm workers, and state and local government employees. Benefits payments for up to 39 weeks significantly increased the antipoverty impact of unemployment insurance.

Workers' Compensation

Workers' compensation, like unemployment insurance, is designed to protect families from poverty during a period when the wages of one of its earners are reduced or interrupted due to work-connected injuries or to tide the family over if the injury is fatal. Besides cash benefits, the system also provides for medical care and rehabilitation of the injured worker.

Workers' compensation is administered in much the same manner as unemployment insurance. In each state there are separate laws and the federal government, railroad, and merchant marine operate separate programs. In recent years, the benefit levels for the disabled have risen substantially. In 26 states during 1979, the maximum weekly benefit for a totally disabled worker was 100 percent or over the average weekly salary in the state. In 23 states the maximum payment equaled or was greater than the cash income required to raise a four-member family out of poverty. Although the rationale for low benefits is that they often encourage a speedy return to work, the level of benefits paid to the totally and permanently disabled and to dependent survivors is not substantially higher than that paid to temporary recipients.

Workers' compensation laws cover approximately 80 percent of the labor force. Farm and domestic workers and other low-earning "casual" workers are excluded from coverage in most states. In 1978 a total of $10 billion was paid in benefits. Most was expended in disability compensation to injured workers, although medical and hospital care accounted for $3.2 billion in payments. An estimated eight of ten recipients of medical care are not off the job long enough to receive cash payments. However, for those requiring medical rehabilitation, the program is reported to be weak. There is no strong linkage between the federal-state vocational rehabilitation program and the workers' compensation system. Instead, vocational services received by the disabled workers are most often the result of efforts by employers and insurance carriers who have a vested interest in restoring the injured worker's productivity.

PRIVATE PENSIONS

Social security benefits alone often leave their elderly recipients near or below the poverty threshold. For a growing proportion of retirees, OASDI is supplemented by benefits from private pension or profit-sharing plans that insure a more adequate standard of living. Though an accurate count of private pensions is not known, it is estimated that over half of all employees in the private sector and most federal, state, and local government employees are covered by a pension or profit-sharing plan. Eligibility requirements have been liberalized significantly over the last decade, increasing the proportion of covered workers ultimately qualifying for retirement benefits. By the end of 1976 it is estimated that 8.3 million beneficiaries—about one of every three retired workers—qualified for some private retirement benefits.

This has important ramifications for poverty among the elderly. Almost all workers covered under private plans are also covered by social security. Most recipients who also qualify for social security are assured of escaping poverty in the "golden years."

Congress enacted the pension reform law in 1974 and has strengthened it since then to safeguard the integrity of private pension funds and to protect the pension rights of employees who change jobs. The private retirement system is a limited antipoverty mechanism. Benefits are paid out of funds accumulated through wage deferrals, and higher-paid workers are more likely to be covered. The private retirement system is a way for middle- and upper-income families to insure against poverty in old age, rather than a way for low-income workers to protect themselves for the future.

TAXING THE POOR

Along with programs providing direct income payments to the poor, several income tax provisions diminish their tax burden and can be viewed, in a sense, as indirect income payments. Tax incentives are becoming increasingly important, but the benefits accruing to the poor account for a small share of the foregone revenue to the federal government.

Of importance to the poor are the additional tax exemptions for aged and blind persons and the tax exclusion of major government income transfer programs. In fiscal 1979 these measures accounted for about one-tenth of the total foregone revenue:

Exclusion of social security benefits	$6.8 billion
Exclusion of unemployment insurance benefits	1.8 billion
Exclusion of public assistance benefits	0.4 billion
Exclusion of veterans' benefits	1.1 billion
Additional exemption for the aged and blind	1.7 billion

Although these amounts are not usually reflected in budget totals, they nonetheless provide substantial benefits to recipients.

The anomaly of the poor paying income taxes while society was trying to raise their income prompted a liberalization of the federal income tax structure. The standard deduction was $2,300 for a single person and $3,400 for married couples. Deductions for personal exemptions were increased to $1,000. To ease the tax burden on low-income persons further, provisions were made to allow a percentage of income as a tax credit of up to $500 for families with dependent children and incomes less than $10,000. The combined effect of these provisions is to exempt a worker with three dependents from paying federal income tax until earnings exceed $7,722 and to create a limited negative income tax for families with incomes below this level.

At the same time, however, other taxes on the poor remain burdensome. The social security tax of 6.13 percent is regressive, even though the upper income limit has been steadily raised. Nor is there any allowance for workers with large families.

State and local sales taxes also pose an increasing burden and do not exempt those on welfare or even the poorest of the poor. Many jurisdictions have sales taxes of 5 percent or more, and some jurisdictions tax food and other necessities.

Indirect taxes also take their toll through utilities bills and rent payments. In some cities, one-quarter or more of rent goes to pay for the landlord's property taxes. Aged homeowners with little income may find property taxes particularly oppressive; according to the Advisory Committee on Intergovernmental Relations, in 1970 nearly 1 million elderly homeowners with incomes below $3,000 spent more than 10 percent of their total money income on property taxes.

Income Maintenance Proposals

Administrative problems, the niggardliness of benefits, gaps in coverage, the rise in costs, and the continued existence of a large number of poor have led to several proposals to supplement or replace existing income maintenance programs with a more comprehensive form of cash assistance. The three basic strategies are (1) either a guaranteed income or negative income tax, (2) children's allowances, and (3) employment guarantees or wage subsidies. The first two are discussed below; public employment and minimum wage provisions are discussed in chapter 5.

Negative Income Tax

The simplest method of eliminating poverty would be to make up the income deficit of the poor in order to guarantee a minimum income. One widely discussed level is the poverty threshold ($7,500 in 1979 dollars) for a family of four. For example, a family of four with an income of $4,000 a year would receive a grant of $3,500. If the family had no income, it would receive $7,500. Such a program would require an estimated $17 billion in payments each year. However, guaranteeing a poverty-level income might reduce the pecuniary incentives to work for millions of people, since their incomes would remain at the poverty threshold whether or not they held jobs. To counter the possibility that such workers would decide to forego employment for the dole, any workable plan must allow low-wage earners to keep at least a portion of their earned income. One proposal would exempt half the earnings of low-income families in qualifying for payments. Thus, a family of four with an income of $4,000 would count only $2,000 for tax purposes and be able to claim $5,500 for a total income of $9,500, compared with the $7,500 maximum paid to family without a wage earner. Such provisions would, of course, increase the cost of the program beyond the amount needed simply to bring all poor people up to the poverty threshold. The magnitude of the cost would depend on the level of incentives offered by the plan. However, it is reasonable to estimate that the annual cost of the plan might rise to at least double the income deficit of the poor needed to bring their income to the poverty threshold. The combination of income support and earnings, proposed by President Carter as part of his welfare reform plans, guaranteed families with children an income equal to 65 percent of the poverty threshold (figure 9).

The income tax structure offers the most convenient vehicle for administering such income guarantees. Though currently geared only to the collection of taxes, the reporting machinery could be adapted to distribute grants and cover income deficits—a negative income tax.

Advocates claim that the negative income tax would substitute a single, comprehensive program of income maintenance for the existing plethora of efforts. Although its simplicity is appealing, the idea does present several problems. Just as the poverty level reflects the fact that it costs more to live in a city and that AFDC payments vary from state to state, the income guarantee should adjust for cost-of-living differentials not only between urban and rural areas but also between various cities and regions. Even more basic is the determination of a family income concept and whether filing units would be altered accordingly.

Figure 9 Proposed income subsidy for a single-parent family of four with $4,654 guaranteed and tax rate of 67 percent after the first $840 of earnings and work expense deduction plus EITC

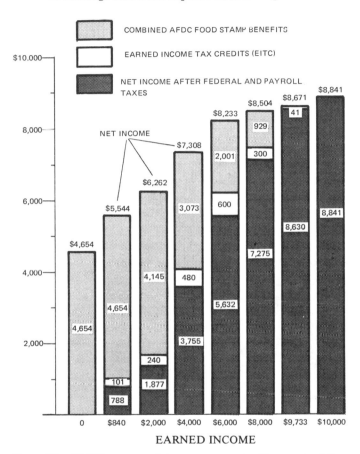

NOTE: The $4,654 guaranteed income represents 65 percent of the poverty threshold based on the OMB poverty level income adjusted for the Department of Agriculture income poverty guidelines.

The timing of payments is also important. Disbursing benefits every April 15 is obviously not often enough. However, paying monthly on the basis of the past month's earnings, for example, may not provide timely relief to a family during a particularly lean period;

paying on the basis of expected earnings may introduce distortions because of inaccurate estimates. The timing of benefits and recertification of eligibility have presented problems under AFDC and will continue to do so under a negative income tax scheme. Futhermore, some mechanism must be retained to provide assistance in emergencies.

A crucial problem in the proposed system is the selection of a base level of benefits and a "marginal tax rate," or the formula by which assistance is reduced as earnings rise. Benefits must be adequate for those who cannot provide for themselves and incentives must be attractive enough to induce the able bodied to contribute to their own support. A low tax rate is of no help to those who cannot work, while a high benefit level may draw able-bodied workers out of the labor market. The availability of unearned benefits may decrease the earnings differential between skilled and unskilled workers and may dampen the incentive to learn skills. Combining a high benefit level with a low tax rate could qualify many middle-income families. Ever present as a constraint on benefits and incentives is the cost of such a program. Taxpayer backlash at the high cost of welfare keeps benefits low.

This tradeoff among benefits, incentives, and cost is present in any public assistance system. There is no "correct" answer, and choosing the best combination remains a question of personal values.

Family Allowances

Another method of providing cash assistance to the poor is to pay families with children a regular allowance to supplement their own incomes and meet some portion of costs of childrearing. This proposal recognizes that the wage system alone distributes income inadequately, because wages are based on productivity or tradition rather than on need. While the principle of equal pay for equal work is desirable as a means of eliminating discrimination based on color, age, or sex, it ignores the differing needs of families and tends to deprive children in large families of basic necessities. The underlying justification for family allowances is that a child's well-being should concern society as a whole.

Our wage system takes little or no account of the diverse needs of workers. Except for adjustments in income taxes, for example, the take-home pay for a bachelor is the same as for the head of a family with dependents in an identical job. Despite the wide acceptance of family allowances in other countries, the idea has never received active consideration in the United States—although it has been advanced on numerous occasions. AFDC is in a sense a form of family allowance, but expenditures under this program accounted for well under 1 percent of national income in 1978. A number of countries spend much more of their national income for family allowances. Family allowances are now paid in all the industrial nations except the United States. These allowances vary widely in benefit patterns, adequacy, and financing. In some countries all children are eligible, while in others no benefits are paid for the first or second child. Benefits are usually paid for children up to the age they would normally leave school, but may be extended for further schooling, training, or apprenticeship. The allowance per child may also vary. For example, Sweden pays a uniform rate for all children, while France has a complex system that adjusts for family income and size and children's ages.

The adequacy of benefits ranges widely. In the United Kingdom the allowance for two children equals 4.4 percent of the average monthly earnings in manufacturing, compared with 16.2 percent in France. For five children, benefits varied from 9.7 percent in Japan to 43.4 percent in France. Just as benefits per child vary from country to country, so does the total magnitude of benefits. As a proportion of the gross national product, expenditures for children's allowances in 1974 ranged from less than 1 percent in West Germany, the United Kingdom, Japan, and Canada to 1.8 percent in Italy and the Netherlands and 2.6 percent in Belgium.

Children's allowance benefits are usually financed by the national government. Many countries reinforce cash outlays with tax deductions for children. Both methods increase a family's resources for rearing children. However, Sweden eliminated the latter when it adopted the former, and the United States has only the latter.

Family allowance programs are not a complete alternative to negative income tax and are certainly no substitute for existing welfare assistance to the aged or to others without children. But because family size is so closely correlated with poverty, family allowances would lift many adults out of poverty along with their children. Family allowances have several advantages over other forms of income maintenance. There is no need for an income test, a feature that would reduce administrative costs and maintain work incentives. Because the program gives benefits to all children, it would probably be more politically acceptable than any alternatives. The major obstacle to family allowances is the belief that, in an era when the dangers of over-population are very real, such a program would encourage procreation. This apparently has not been the case in other countries with such programs, and in any event childbearing would not be a profitable enterprise under any of the programs that have any chance of passage. Nonetheless, family allowances should be coupled with effective birth control programs to reduce the potential number of unwanted children.

Pending Welfare Proposals

Reflecting dissatisfaction with current operations of the welfare system, a number of alternatives have been proposed and debated in recent years. A few vital issues have emerged: the level of assistance, incentives and requirements to work, and the overlap with in-kind benefits. The costs to taxpayers embodied in the various proposals are also a crucial consideration in selecting alternatives to aid the poor.

Most of the suggestions covered all families with children, thus adding to AFDC families the "working poor" but not the poor without children. However, one proposal would have added a "demogrant," or payment to each person, regardless of family status. Instead of the fragmented AFDC program, in which each state operated independently but with federal contributions, the federal government would establish a uniform minimum nationwide benefit schedule. Proposed benefit levels ranged from half of the poverty threshold to 50 percent above it. The lower level of support would have constituted an increase over AFDC payments in only a few states. However, the states would not be prevented from supplementing the federal payments. The maximum proposal would have included a broad chunk of the populace and would have been extremely expensive. In some versions the payment was solely a transfer, but in other proposals public service jobs would be available at low rates of pay to supplement low base payments.

Determining who was employable and whether employable family members should be encouraged or required to work was another stumbling block. The most lenient proposals included no coercion, allowing welfare mothers to choose whether to stay home with their children or go to work, and offered attractive incentives to work, permitting recipients to keep up to two-thirds of their earnings. Others envisioned harsh requirements that recipients find employment, take make-work jobs, or undergo training, and included paltry work incentives of as little as one-third of earnings.

Meshing cash assistance with existing in-kind programs presented two thorny problems. First, each program provided that benefits be reduced as earnings increased. These reductions, however, were not coordinated, so the cumulative "marginal tax rates" for the several programs sometimes approached or even exceeded 100 percent. This meant that recipients *lost* economic benefits by working more. Second, some variations disqualified recipients of cash relief from obtaining certain in-kind benefits. The increased cash, it was argued, would more than substitute for loss of food stamps. But this was not always true. Not only would some families gain only a few dollars to compensate for the loss of several hundred dollars in in-kind benefits, but other families, in states paying more than the federal minimum, would lose the in-kind aid and receive nothing at all in return.

The Carter administration's 1980 welfare reform proposal offered a middle ground on these issues in an attempt to combine welfare with work. After the proposed Better Jobs and Income program, which advocated a sweeping reform of the welfare system at an estimated annual cost of an additional $17 billion (1977 dollars), failed to gather congressional support, the administration proposed a more incremental approach as a workable compromise. Taking one more step toward guaranteed income for all poor families with children, the bill proposed changes in benefit levels and eligibility criteria that would reduce inequalities in the present system and provide a minimum support level of combined AFDC and food stamp benefits at 65 percent of the poverty level income. The earned income tax credit would also be boosted (see figure 9). A family of four with a monthly income of less than $500 would have been eligible to receive welfare assistance. To overcome incentives to quit work in order to join welfare rolls, the bill provided for the same deductions in earnings in determining eligibility as were permitted to families already on the rolls.

Though work disincentives would be reduced, work incentives, to a large extent, would be dependent on intensive job search requirements and job creation and training programs. Starting initially with a proposal that would have virtually guaranteed jobs to all welfare recipients capable of work, the administration retreated to a less ambitious plan that would provide work opportunities and, to a limited extent, training to only a portion of welfare recipients and potential recipients.

The rapid growth of food stamps, Medicaid, supplemental security income, and unemployment benefits has increased the number of variables to be considered in reform. A debate with so many combatants and so many issues could result in legislation only after considerable political compromise. Of particular significance in the legislative debates is the fact that income maintenance is recognized as a federal responsibility and that guaranteed income for at least part of the population is now a viable potential issue. The feasibility of combining work and welfare has also gained wide acceptance and is close to becoming a politically acceptable approach to welfare reform.

ADDITIONAL READINGS

Aaron, Henry J. *Why Is Welfare So Hard to Reform?* Washington, D.C.: Brookings Institution, 1973.

Ball, Robert M. *Social Security: Today and Tomorrow.* New York: Columbia University Press, 1978.

Levitan, Sar A.; Rein, Martin; and Marwick, David. *Work and Welfare Go Together.* Baltimore: Johns Hopkins University Press, 1976.

Munnell, Alicia H. *The Future of Social Security.* Washington, D.C.: Brookings Institution, 1977.

Salamon, Lester M. *Welfare, the Elusive Consensus.* New York: Praeger Publishers, 1978.

Stein, Bruno. *Social Security and Provisions in Transition.* New York: Free Press, 1980.

U.S. Congressional Budget Office. *Welfare Reform: Issues, Objectives, and Approaches.* Washington, D.C.: Government Printing Office, 1977.

DISCUSSION QUESTIONS

1. How do you explain the growth of AFDC during the prosperous latter half of the 1960s while the number on the rolls remained relatively stable during the following decade when unemployment rose?

2. OASDI, unemployment insurance, and AFDC reduce poverty and alleviate deprivation. Compare the strengths and weaknesses of the approaches underlying each of these programs as part of concerted antipoverty measures.

3. Less than 1 percent of total national income distributed among the poor would raise them all to the poverty threshold and thus alleviate poverty. If it appears that the price tag is so low, why hasn't the United States taken the necessary steps to eradicate poverty?

4. Why do you think there are separate veterans' programs based on needs tests?

5. "The negative income tax is the most efficient and equitable means of dealing with the poverty problem in the United States. With such a scheme, most welfare programs would become unnecessary." Discuss.

6. Examine the trends and empirical data bearing on the thesis that there has been a growing interdependence between work and income maintenance. Outline the major ingredients of an income support policy that would do the least damage to work incentives.

3

Provision of Services and Goods

For I was hungry and you gave me food, I was thirsty and you gave me drink, I
    was a stranger and you welcomed me,
I was naked and you clothed me, I was sick and you visited me, I was in
    prison and you came to me.

—Matthew 25:35–36

The provision of aid to the poor is not limited to cash assistance. While
the Great Society and subsequent legislation has expanded income
support for the poor, the major thrust of the assistance provided to the
poor in the 1970s was dominated by the provision of goods and
services. The latter accounted for three-fifths of total outlays in 1980,
as compared to one-fifth of outlays in 1964 (figure 10). In this sense,
the welfare state has grown to unprecedented scope and diversity,
providing both necessities—such as medical care, food, and shelter—
and supportive services designed to improve the quality of life of poor
people .

The heavy reliance on providing goods and services for the poor
can be traced to a deep and longstanding public skepticism concerning
the moral character and reliability of poor people. In its most cynical
form, this skepticism is expressed in a view of the poor as lazy and
dishonest, beating the system and thriving on government hand-outs.
Even those less suspicious of the poor often question their ability to
manage their own resources responsibly, and prefer goods and

Figure 10 Per capita cash and in-kind assistance for the poor (1979 dollars)

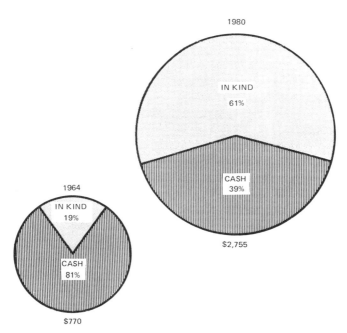

services that meet their real needs over cash assistance which the poor might squander. These perceptions of the poor lend political support to in-kind approaches to aid the poor that seem to minimize the risk of fraud or waste. But even those who favor extending maximum flexibility to the poor and providing them cash assistance find that in the absence of government intervention needed services and facilities are not available to the poor either because of their isolation or because of shortcomings in the market mechanisms.

The relative merits of cash and in-kind assistance can be debated at length, but it is important to note that even the federal provision of goods and services offers some flexibility for the poor. While some services (for example, compensatory education) are provided directly by the government, many others are offered through a system of payments and reimbursements that includes a broad range of service providers. Thus, most health care for the poor is provided indirectly, with all three levels of government sharing the cost and with some opportunity for the poor to choose their own physicians rather than depending solely on care available in public institutions. By covering the cost of specific goods and services, these payments differ significantly from general income supplements, yet they allow more freedom of choice than the direct government provision of basic necessities.

As part of an overview of programs in aid of the poor, this chapter focuses primarily on goods and services made available by the federal government on the basis of need. A broader study would show that the federal role in the provision of goods and services extends far beyond these antipoverty efforts, that most of their benefits are dispensed without regard to the recipients' level of income, and that they cost far more than all programs expressly designed for the poor. For example, educating the nation's children and youth alone costs nearly twice as much as all federal programs targeted directly at the poor. The magnitude of aid to the nonpoor is illustrated even more clearly in what the late Richard M. Titmuss called the "iceberg phenomenon of social welfare," the revenue system that exempts certain types of expenditures from income taxes. (The provision allowing homeowners to deduct interest on home mortgages from taxable income is a typical example.) Therefore, even in the context of a discussion of those goods and services directed to the poor, it must be recognized that many direct public services—as well as "fiscal welfare" provisions— tend to favor the affluent members of society over the poor.

MEDICAL SERVICES

The linkage between poverty and poor health has long been recognized, and medical services are now considered by our society as an essential ingredient of even a minimum standard of living. Since the passage of Medicare and Medicaid in 1965 the federal government has assumed the major responsibility as the provider of health care for the aged and the poor. The estimated 1980 federal contribution to health care programs in aid of the poor amounted to more than $16 billion.

	millions
Total	*$16,174*
Medicare	5,041
Medicaid	9,323
Community Health Projects	776
Veterans	512
Maternal and Child Health	189
Indians	311
Other	22

Note: The total figure differs from others cited in the text because of different sources and methods of estimating the data. No exact figures are available.

Despite these massive public expenditures, the deficit in health care for the poor remains startling, whether measured in life expectancy, infant mortality rates, or numbers of visits to physicians or dentists. Considering the expanding government outlays, what accounts for the deficiencies in health care? No doubt some of the funds are wasted by inept administration; and as in other areas, the health costs of the poor are higher, especially when the government foots the bill. However, waste and overcharges reflect only part of the reason for soaring federal expenditures in health care and slow rates of health improvement. The following factors account for the persisting health deficiencies of the poor, and suggest that rapid improvements at a reasonable cost may remain elusive:

1. The poor, on the average, require more medical attention than the general population, because of the very health conditions (advanced age, or physical or mental handicaps) that keep many of them out of work force and unable to secure adequate income.

2. Preventative health care for the poor is almost nonexistent. In addition to the nutritional deficiencies and environmental health risks facing the poor, the subsidized health care system itself only encourages delay in treatment of health problems until they develop into major crises. With federal funds for the health care of poor children extremely limited, the prospects for improvements in preventative health care are slim.

3. The delivery system for health services, generally inefficient in America, is particularly disorganized and inadequate in serving the poor. Shortages of medical and allied health personnel have retarded the development of adequate health services in neighborhoods where

economic incentives are limited, and yet the alternative of community health services is typically fragmented and often inaccessible.

Medicare and Medicaid

The federal government's most important health care programs are Medicare and Medicaid, both added to the Social Security Act in 1965. Medicare covers the bulk of hospital and medical costs of persons who are 65 years of age and older and disabled social security beneficiaries. All social security and railroad retirement recipients and others who meet special qualifications are entitled to hospital insurance (HI). In 1980, 27.4 million persons were covered, and about 6.4 million received hospital care. HI pays a major part of costs of up to 90 days of hospitalization, as well as posthospital extended care and home health services.

All persons entitled to HI benefits, as well as retired federal employees, are also eligible for supplementary medical insurance (SMI) to help pay the cost of doctors' and surgeons' fees, diagnostic tests, medical supplies, and prescription drugs. To participate in this plan, the enrollee pays a $9.60 monthly premium that is matched by the federal government. In 1980 about 17.4 million persons—nearly two-thirds of those eligible—were served.

Perhaps the greatest criticism of the SMI program is that the plan's premium costs discourage many aged near-poor from participating. In addition to the monthly premium, individuals enrolled in the program also pay a $60 annual deductible, bringing the recipient's out-of-pocket cost to $175 per year before SMI contributions become available. Even then the enrollee is responsible for 20 percent of all remaining costs. States are required to pay premiums, deductibles, and the 20 percent of uncovered costs for the elderly people receiving supplementary security income payments. People who are "medically needy"—those whose incomes are barely above the poverty threshold—must pay their own premiums, although states may pay deductibles and additional out-of-pocket costs. However, only relatively few states and the District of Columbia provide these benefits for their elderly medically needy population.

While Medicare is a universal program designed to help the elderly regardless of their income, about 15 percent of Medicare outlays benefit the elderly poor. No doubt the Medicare program has kept many near-poor elderly out of poverty, and has eased the anxieties of those elderly whose life savings would have been wiped out as the result of a major illness.

Of more direct benefit to the poor is Medicaid. Persons receiving federally supported public assistance in all states except Arizona are eligible, and 32 states and the District of Columbia extend eligibility to persons who do not qualify for public assistance but whose income is sufficiently low to qualify them as "medically needy." In 1980, the federal contribution to medical services for nearly 23 million persons via Medicaid totaled $14.2 billion, two-thirds of which aided persons below the poverty threshold. Despite Medicare benefits, persons over 65 years of age continue to receive a larger portion of Medicaid funds than any other recipient group (figure 11).

Medicaid was launched in 1965 to replace a fragmented system of medical assistance to recipients of separate public assistance programs. It offers reimbursements to states for a portion of the medical costs of low-income persons including public assistance and SSI recipients, with the federal share of expenses ranging from 50 to 78 percent, depending upon the scope of services and eligibility requirements. Each state administers and operates its own programs, setting its own rules within the confines of federal guidelines and regulations. In 1968 Congress restricted Medicaid to families with an income of no more than one-third above the AFDC income cut-off—a step taken because several states had set significantly higher income ceilings. Ceilings in 1978 ranged from $1,296 to $3,600 for individuals and from $2,400 to $6,600 for a family of four.

The dominant theme in the development of both Medicare and Medicaid programs—as well as in-kind assistance programs in shelter, food, and social services—has been the attempt to contain program costs. In the early stages of these programs, efforts to improve the quality of medical services for the poor led to federal requirements that states set standards for the reimbursement of hospitals and physicians at prevailing local rates. However, in order to allay fears of "socialized medicine," no provision was made for federal monitoring of reimbursements, and charges of program fraud haunted both Medicare and Medicaid. By the early 1970s, stories of

Figure 11 Medicaid, 1980

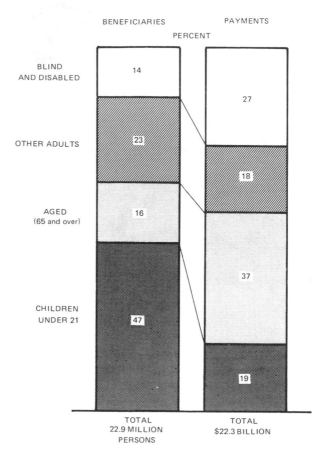

SOURCE: U.S. Department of Health and Human Services

"Medicaid mills" with physicians claiming reimbursement for as many as 150 patients in a single day drew careful federal review of medical programs for the poor.

The federal response to rising program costs and continuing reports of fraud and abuse in Medicare and Medicaid has been far from swift. Congress sought to remedy such unethical behavior and to tighten the law requiring the payment of "reasonable cost" by directing HEW to spell out standards controlling the reimbursement of hospitals and physicians under Medicare, Medicaid, and maternal and child health programs. Self-regulation remained virtually in effect, however, leaving the administration of Medicaid and other federal health care programs loosely monitored until concern over abuse of federal health programs resulted in 1972 in congressionally mandated institution of professional standards review organizations (PSROs) representing local practitioners to monitor Medicare and Medicaid services. The PSROs also fell short of their aim. It was not until 1977 that they became fully operational, and comprehensive studies have found that they have little impact on the costs of federal health care programs.

Federal pursuit of program fraud and abuse continues into the 1980s—both the 94th and 95th congresses enacted legislation to facilitate and prosecute such violations. The findings of the newly created Office of the Inspector General in HEW that an estimated 7 percent of federal outlays to Medicare and Medicaid were lost to fraud and abuse have only fueled congressional concern. Ultimately, there is little reason to believe that such overcharges, even if disturbing, are the driving force behind skyrocketing program costs. The reluctance of Congress to restrict increases in hospital revenues and expenditures is probably a more potent contributor to the growing cost of public health services than the ineffectiveness of measures to control abuses of Medicare and Medicaid.

Community Health Projects

Given the expansion of federal outlays for the health care of the poor, the challenge of improving medical care and the efficiency of the health industry in delivering services to the poor became paramount. In the efforts to develop long-range solutions to the problems of poverty, it was virtually inevitable that programs initiated during the Great Society would experiment with the means to respond to this emerging need. Assuming that improving the health of the poor required not only massive funds but also a major restructuring of the health care delivery system, the Office of Economic Opportunity established neighborhood health centers with four basic goals: (1) to provide a full range of ambulatory health services; (2) to maintain a close liaison with other community services; (3) to develop close

65

working relationships with a hospital (preferably one with a medical school affiliation); and (4) to foster the participation of the indigenous population in decisionmaking and employment in the centers.

As the most important effort to restructure the health care system in poor neighborhoods, the OEO neighborhood health centers represented a landmark of federal health care policy. However, compared with other government contributions to medical services for the poor, the outlays for health centers were no more than a proverbial drop in the bucket. Even after the dismantling of the antipoverty agency, federal support for health centers has continued, totaling $320 million in 1980 and maintaining 632 community health centers (including 442 rural health projects).

Veterans

A variety of other programs provide subsidized health care for the poor, most of them concentrating on specific groups, (i.e., Indians, veterans, migrants, or handicapped children). The most important of these is the medical program for veterans.

The Veterans Administration health care system, originally designed to care for war wounded, currently provides free care on a broad scale to aged and indigent veterans whose medical needs are in no way related to military service. All "medically indigent" war veterans are eligible for VA hospital care, and most of the patients in VA hospitals have no service-connected injury. The criteria for eligibility are based not on set income limitations but on the individual's opinion of what he can afford.

The VA expended $6.4 billion on medical care in 1980. The system operates 172 hospitals, 91 nursing care units, 16 domiciliaries, and 220 outpatient clinics. The VA also contributes to the cost of care received by veterans in state-run domiciliaries and nursing homes.

In considering the impact of the VA health care system in aiding the poor, the parallels between the VA and Medicare programs are striking. By using eligibility criteria not strictly related to poverty, both health care programs fail to bring aid efficiently to the most needy. Yet even in the absence of a highly targeted program structure, many of the aged served by Medicare and the veterans served by the VA system are indeed poor. With the recognition that both programs also serve as "safety nets" that keep the near-poor from economic disaster when costly illness strikes, the case for using VA and Medicare programs as vehicles for aid to the poor becomes, if not persuasive, at least more understandable.

Native Americans

The American Indian living on a reservation and the Alaskan native are perhaps the most poverty-stricken minorities in the country, and the American health care system offers these groups only limited relief. With about three-fifths of all American Indians living on isolated reservations and most native Alaskans residing in inland villages, their geographic and economic settings rarely attract private health facilities. Poor roads and inadequate transportation and communication heighten these barriers to health care, creating serious problems for individuals hampered by illness. Although native Americans are eligible for Medicaid, even its impact is diminished by geographic location—about one-fourth of the reservation population resides in Arizona, the only state not participating in Medicaid programs.

In this context, it is clear that both isolation and poverty take their tolls. Indians have the nation's highest incidence of tuberculosis and suffer disproportionately from streptococcal infections, nutritional and dental deficiencies, poor mental health, and attendant disorders. Alaskan natives fare only slightly better in major health indices. It is this dramatic result of isolation and poverty that created a mandate for special health services under the auspices of the U.S. Department of Health and Human Services.

The Indian Health Service in HHS meets some of these medical needs, employing some 10,000 health care personnel in 48 federally operated hospitals and 49 outpatient clinics located on or near reservations. Contracted services are also acquired in nonfederal facilities. The purchase of care for over 75,000 hospital admissions, 3.1 million visitors to outpatient and mental health clinics, visiting health workers' services, and facility construction and renovation accounted for the $538 million expenditure by the Indian Health Service in 1980.

Measured in terms of progress in lessening the tremendous health deficit of Indians, the efforts of the Indian Health Service over recent decades have resulted in considerable progress. Between 1950 and

1970 the life expectancy of Indians increased 5.1 years. Between 1960 and 1977, the Indian death rate from influenza and pneumonia decreased 67 percent. The infant mortality rate has dropped from 61 to 18 deaths per 1,000 live births. Family-planning services are rendered to more than two-fifths of the female population between 15 and 44 years of age and consequently, the birth rate per 1,000 people has dropped from 37 to 31 births. There has been a decline in the number of new tuberculosis cases and the deaths caused by that disease.

However, despite the progress achieved under the Indian Health Service, facilities remain primitive compared with sophisticated city hospitals, and the service lacks adequate and experienced personnel. As long as doctors could be drafted and their military requirements fulfilled by working on reservations, a sufficient supply of physicians was available. In the absence of the draft, shortages have developed. Turnover of other personnel contributes to the persisting cultural gaps between the health workers and the target population. More extensive training of Indian health personnel would help alleviate these deficiencies and create a health labor pool with roots in the community. In order to improve the health of the native American population, underlying deficiencies in housing, nutrition, and health education must also be corrected.

SHELTER

On the average, 15 percent of consumer expenditures are for rent or home ownership costs and 7 percent more are for furnishings and equipment. Given the high and rising cost of shelter, both old and new, poor families are faced with grim choices: they can live in substandard units, they can economize on space by crowding into dwellings that are more adequate, or they can use a disproportionate share of their meager incomes for housing. In many cases, they must resort to all three. Out of the 80.7 million unit, year-round housing stock in 1977, 2.5 million units lacked plumbing facilities and as many as several million units were dilapidated and in need of major repairs. In the same year, there were 3.3 million occupied units with more than one person per room—the accepted American standard for overcrowding.

Close to half of renter families had to spend more than one-fourth of their income for shelter and utilities.

Federal policies have contributed significantly to the alleviation of the nation's housing problems. The broader approach has been to promote the construction of new homes for middle-income families, hoping to open vacancies for lower-income renters and home buyers. Roughly 18 percent of all mortgage loans for private homes in 1978 were guaranteed by the Federal Housing Administration, the Veterans Administration, or the Farmers Home Administration. Savings to homeowners and rental property owners from special tax treatment amounted to about $16 billion. All these forms of assistance stimulate housing construction, and though the poor receive only a minute proportion of this aid, they may benefit from the "trickle down" effect. The more than 80 percent decline in substandard housing between 1960 and 1977 and the 43 percent increase in housing over the same period of time were in part the result of federal incentives and aids for new construction.

Of more direct importance to the poor, however, are the various federal programs that subsidize the building, rental, leasing, purchase, and operation of apartments and houses for low-income households. At the end of fiscal 1980, there were approximately 3.7 million units available for occupancy, involving an annual subsidy of over $5 billion (table 3). Three-fourths of these units were produced since 1968.

The oldest and one of the largest housing assistance programs to the poor is public housing. Initiated in 1937, the public housing program provides federal subsidies for the amortization of construction costs on units built, owned, and operated by local housing authorities. The units are reserved for low-income families, with locally established income limits that cannot exceed 72 percent of the median income level in the area. With the federal subsidy to cover capital costs, rents need to cover only the operating expense; typically, they are between one-half and one-third less than market rates for similar units. Some of the poor are unable to pay even this low rent without using more than one-fourth of their adjusted incomes. Since 1969, the federal government has been authorized to make up the difference between operating costs and what tenants can reasonably pay (which is not to

Table 3. Federally subsidized housing units ready for occupancy, 1980

	Units (in thousands)	Annual expenditures (in millions)
Total	*3,730*	*$5,432*
Housing Assistance Payments (Section 8)	1,141	2,055
Public housing including leased	1,192	1,277
Rent Supplement	178	268
Interest rate subsidies for home ownership (235)	204	105
Interest rate subsidies for rentals (236)	538	647
Elderly	75	700
Rehabilitation loans	126	215
Farmers Home Administration programs	276	170

Source: U.S. Departments of Housing and Urban Development and Agriculture.

exceed 30 percent of a household's adjusted income), in addition to the capital amortization subsidy.

From the inception of direct federal housing aid during the 1930s until the new programs were initiated under the Great Society, public housing was the mainstay of efforts to ensure shelter for the poor. Even throughout the 1970s, public housing brought highly targeted assistance to the poor, often working in tandem with other public assistance programs. Of the families that moved in or were reexamined for continued occupancy in the year ending September 30, 1978, four-fifths were receiving some kind of low-income assistance or benefits. More than two-thirds of the families had no one working. Nearly two-fifths of the households were headed by an elderly person. The median income for all the families was about $3,718 and they paid a median annual rent of $750.

This greatest strength of public housing—its highly targeted aid to the poor—has also generated the program's greatest political liability. As became apparent in the 1960s, the building and operating of housing for low-income families is a massive undertaking that can be very expensive. The estimated average cost for a new unit of public housing in 1980 was over $57,000, with an average annual federal cost for construction and financing of $5,340 per unit. In 1980, there were a total of 1,192,000 public housing units operated at an annual capital subsidy of $1,071 per unit, not including an operating subsidy of an additional $687 per unit. As construction and operating costs (including fuel and utility expenses) continue to rise, the burden of public housing expenditures can only be expected to increase in the future.

Coupled with the rising costs over the past two decades, public housing has been plagued by a number of difficulties. To save costs and to avoid political opposition, many public housing units were located in large-scale, inner-city projects. The concentration of poor families in deteriorating neighborhoods has led to problems of vandalism, crime, and general malaise among tenants. Facing such broad problems and a serious shortage of funds, many central city housing authorities have had no choice but to let their units deteriorate. Additional operating subsidies approved by Congress in 1970 saved some local housing authorities from collapse. In 1979, the Housing and Community Development Amendments included special provisions for public housing modernization and aid to troubled projects, yet if past practice is any indicator of future action, congressional appropriation will certainly fall far short of the cost of even necessary improvements. In many areas, public housing is still far short of a "decent home and suitable living environment," though it is still better than alternatives available to the poor, as long waiting lists attest.

The difficulties experienced with public housing led to a host of new programs launched during the Great Society era of the 1960s. In the broadest sense, the new approaches tested in the 1960s marked a shift from a reliance on the direct provision of housing to the use of indirect federal subsidies designed to help the poor afford housing in the private market. In experimenting with these subsidy and incentive programs, the critics of public housing hoped to disperse low-income families beyond the confines of poor neighborhoods and to contain federal housing costs by relying on existing housing stock. Public housing efforts were not abandoned, but beginning in 1964 the range of federal housing options increased dramatically.

The earliest attempt to shift low-income families into privately owned units differed little from public housing itself. The Housing and Urban Development Act of 1964 authorized subsidies to local housing authorities for the lease of privately owned units, with eligible families then paying public housing rents. The effort to promote dispersal of public housing projects also led to the creation of a rent supplement program in 1965, providing subsidies to bridge the gap between market rents and one-fourth of the tenant's adjusted income. Both the leasing and rent supplement programs were based on a hope that rent-subsidized units could be sprinkled among unsubsidized housing. Neither one achieved much success in this area. In the absence of suburban cooperation in expanding housing opportunities for the poor, the overwhelming majority of leased units remain in low-income neighborhoods. Rent supplements may have had more potential for promoting dispersal, but the skyrocketing operating costs of other federally assisted housing have forced a "piggybacking" of rent supplements with other housing subsidies to keep rent levels within the reach of low-income households. Thus, in 1980, most of the 178,000 units covered under the rent supplement program were in completely rent-supplemented projects, or were used along with other subsidy programs to reach an even lower-income clientele.

The Housing and Urban Development Act of 1968 added two more subsidy programs that became for a while the primary focus of activity. Again, the intent of Congress was to move away from public housing and toward a greater reliance on the private sector. In retrospect, the forces working against the poor in the private housing market were more powerful than had been hoped or expected.

One approach, known as the "236" program (corresponding to the appropriate section of the act), provides subsidies to lenders so that the interest rate on privately owned low-income rental housing projects can be reduced to 1 percent. However, since the rents must cover the operating costs plus capital repayment costs, the rents are higher and the tenants must have a higher income level. To offset the higher rents built into the 236 program, many of the units are also covered by the rent supplement program. In 1980 close to two-thirds of the 538,000 units assisted by the 236 program were receiving rent supplements. The median annual income of those who moved in during 1978 was $6,361, $2,643 higher than for public housing tenants. More than two-thirds of the families had at least one person working. Less than 20 percent were headed by elderly persons.

The 235 homeownership program seeks to help lower-income families become property owners by requiring lower down payments and providing interest rate subsidies to hold down the cost of mortgage payments. The number of units covered by the program reached a peak of 419,000 in 1974 after the Nixon administration terminated new commitments under the program. The program was resumed in 1975, but by 1980 the number of units covered by the 235 subsidies was less than half what it was in 1974. Similar to the 236 program,

235 homeowner assistance has had difficulties reaching the poor. Under the 1976 revisions, effective for all subsequent subsidies, any family with an adjusted gross income up to 95 percent of the area median income is eligible to receive assistance under this program. Though additional subsidies are available to families whose monthly mortgage, insurance, and tax payments exceed 20 percent of their income, the required minimum down payment of 3 percent of acquisition costs and ongoing expenditures on upkeep prevent many households below the poverty level from participating. The average initial investment of 235 recipients in 1978 was over $2,000. The median annual family income was $11,990, and virtually no recipient had an income less than $6,000 annually—still above the poverty level then for a family of four.

Although the housing programs have assuredly succeeded in making some decent housing affordable to the poor, the overall record was not without serious flaws. The objective of dispersing subsidized housing out of concentrated pockets in urban centers has not been met. Local resistance to spreading low-cost housing and piggybacked programs has limited the reach of the programs to smaller areas and fewer persons than would probably be possible otherwise. The unexpectedly large and growing commitment for operating subsidies mandates alternative solutions for the long run.

The Housing and Community Development Act of 1974 cut back the strong federal role in establishing a national housing policy by stressing community block grants to be spent according to broad guidelines. In an effort to relieve some of the nonproductive maintenance expenses for upkeep of vacant federally owned housing units, the act authorized HUD to transfer to local housing authorities small (one to four units) residential dwellings. They are sold at nominal cost to poor or near-poor persons under an urban homesteading program. The act also authorized a new rental assistance program and conventional public housing construction, in addition to assistance for the elderly.

The most significant single program established by the Housing and Community Development Act of 1974 is Section 8, the Housing Assistance Payments program. In its most basic form, Section 8 is an expanded rent supplement program offering broad flexibility with regard to the type of unit receiving rent subsidy. Units can be publicly or privately owned (although not in public housing projects), with an emphasis on private ownership. There is no direct assistance for either construction or permanent financing, but indirect aid in financing may be obtained through state housing finance agencies or local public housing authorities.

For local communities, Section 8 housing offers new opportunities to shape federal block grant aid to match local conditions and needs. For recipients of rent subsidies, Section 8 also provides a greater choice of location and housing type, with the hope of greater racial and income integration. Households with incomes below 80 percent of the median in their area are eligible for assistance. Those with incomes under 50 percent pay between 15 and 25 percent of their income in rent, and those with slightly higher incomes can be required to pay up to a maximum of 30 percent of their incomes. The federal government pays the difference between the tenant's payment and a contract rent. The median income for families moving into Section 8 housing in early 1979 was $3,690, one-fifth of the median family income in the nation. Three-fourths of the recipients had incomes less than $5,000. After less than six years of operation, by 1980 the Section 8 program included well over a million subsidized units and funds reserved for nearly 500,000 future units, rapidly overtaking public housing as the major federal program offering housing assistance to the poor.

The federal government is still committed to supporting construction of lower-income housing and subsidizing and underwriting interest costs for private construction for low-income tenants. However, by 1980, although the 1949 pledge of "a decent home and suitable living environment for every American family" was not formally abandoned, inflationary trends threatened to reverse the earlier gains of federal housing policy. The emphasis in housing—as in other social action areas—is on returning the strategy initiative to the market and down to the local level. Whether community officials will continue to make good use of the federal dollar will only be borne out by time.

Aside from assuming a direct financial burden, Congress has taken legislative action beyond the open housing laws in attempting to alter the structural elements of the housing market itself. While as yet unwilling to outlaw "redlining" (the practice of refusing to make loans to certain urban neighborhoods regardless of personal credit worthiness), the Congress did enact legislation in 1975 to discourage the practice by forcing lending institutions to disclose the amounts of mortgage money they lend to different areas of a city. More recently, the Department of Housing and Urban Development has begun attempts to challenge exclusionary zoning policies of affluent communities in the courts, and to question local compliance with federal equal opportunity housing statutes administratively as a condition for receipt of federal community development and recreation funds. While the intensity of future efforts in this area is impossible to predict, it would not be surprising if legal and administrative challenges to institutional barriers to low-income housing took greater prominence in federal housing efforts. Without these basic structural changes, even massive infusion of federal funds through existing housing programs could do little to promote the dispersal of low-income units that is so vital to the future of the poor.

HOUSEHOLD ENERGY

Fuel and weatherization assistance for low-income households represents a new extension of the welfare state. Policies designed to help the poor heat their homes have been initiated in response to rising costs of fuel and reflect an expanded concept of basic needs. During the first six years following the initial OPEC cartel boost of oil prices, the cost of fuel nearly tripled, while total consumer prices rose by about 60 percent. In 1970 home energy costs represented about 9 percent of the entire income for low-income households and about 3 percent for the average American household. By 1980, home energy costs for a low-income household represented about 20 percent of their entire income compared to 7 percent for the average American household.

President Carter also decided in 1979 to decontrol the price of domestic oil. The theory behind this policy decision is that if domestic oil prices rise to the higher level in international markets, then American consumers will be forced to decrease their energy demands while producers will increase domestic supplies. However, a major side effect of this policy is that it will vastly increase the burden poor households face in meeting their basic energy needs.

To help remedy this plight the federal government inaugurated programs to help low-income households conserve energy and to help offset a part of the energy price hikes. Starting in 1975 with an initial modest low-income home weatherization program of roughly $17 million, the price tag grew to $200 million two years later. Families with incomes below 125 percent of the poverty threshold are eligible for assistance. The Department of Energy allocates weatherization funds to the states based on a formula that considers local temperatures and heating requirements, and the estimated number of low-income households. In 1979 the maximum grant expenditure per dwelling was $800, but state advisory councils could obtain Department of Energy authority to allocate more per dwelling under certain conditions.

With domestic decontrol of oil prices, and as part of the Crude Oil Windfall Profit Tax Act of 1980, the federal government initiated a program to cover the heating needs of the poor and near-poor. As an interim effort Congress appropriated $1.6 billion for fiscal 1980. Of this total, $400 million was allocated for the Energy Crisis Assistance Programs (ECAP), administered by the Community Services Administration. ECAP provided emergency assistance to households with incomes no higher than 125 percent of the poverty threshold. The funds had to be used for the payment of energy-related costs, and they could not be used for weatherization. No more than $400 could be spent on a household. If a state set a higher level it had to provide a portion of the funds to make up this difference. Another $400 million was allocated for a special one-time energy allowance, not exceeding $250 per person, for recipients of Supplemental Security Income. Finally, $800 million was to be distributed to states as block grants. The states could pick from several plans in spending these funds. A state could provide a lump sum payment to all AFDC recipients, or develop a plan to provide assistance to populations other than AFDC recipients. The states could also transfer the funds to community action programs, or they could develop their own plan. The allocation formula to give federal funds to the states was based on local climate and the number of low-income households. Of the $1.6 billion more than two-thirds was spent on the poor.

Lasting federal legislation to aid the poor in energy-related costs was contained in the Crude Oil Windfall Profit Tax Act of 1980. Title III, known as the Home Energy Assistance Act of 1980, authorized over $3 billion for this program in fiscal 1981. About 95 percent of the funds will be allocated to states based on formulas that take into consideration local energy expenditures and the number of low-income households, and most of the remaining balance will be allocated to the CSA. Households receiving AFDC, SSI, food stamps, and certain veterans' assistance, or any household that has an income below the lower living standard established by BLS, are eligible to receive energy assistance.

Under this act Congress has determined that part of the windfall profit from higher energy prices should be returned to the poor. This program is slated to remain in effect as long as the federal government continues to collect part of the windfall energy profits.

FOOD

The federal role in the provision of food to the poor reflects a relatively new commitment to in-kind assistance. While the federal food stamp program was in operation nationally from 1939 to 1943, the program was not revived as a source of in-kind aid to the poor until 1961. Similarly, the diverse child nutrition programs were not launched until the Great Society era of the 1960s with the creation of the school lunch, school breakfast, and special milk programs. Yet, after a slow beginning with federal food expenditures in the 1960s, the succeeding decade witnessed a massive growth in federal spending for direct food assistance to the poor, reaching a total of $12.6 billion by 1980 (figure 12).

This dramatic expansion of food programs was the result of a highly diverse political coalition with very different interests and concerns. Some saw food programs as a way of getting more for the poor by raising the cry of "hunger in America." Others favored food distribution because they were concerned that the poor would use their cash grants unwisely. Still others sought to sustain the demand for certain agricultural products. Yet the result was a strong and repeated preference in American public policy for providing food directly to the poor instead of allocating a portion of their cash assistance to food, and a corresponding growth in the federal network of in-kind assistance programs. Over 90 percent of all benefits under these food programs are distributed on the basis of need, and perhaps more than in any other in-kind aid program the poor receive an overwhelming share of this federal assistance.

77

Figure 12 Food assistance, 1972 and 1980

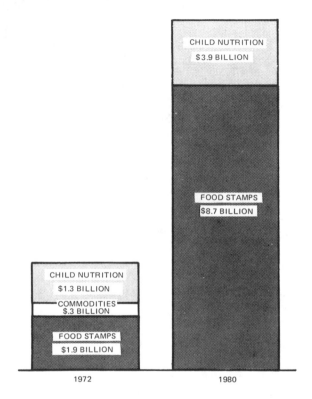

SOURCE: U.S. Office of Management and Budget

Food Stamps

By far the largest of federal food subsidies, the food stamp program in 1980 increased the purchasing power of nearly 20 million persons at a cost of about $8.7 billion annually (figure 13). Under this program, households receive monthly allotments of food stamps, based on their income and household size, which can be exchanged in retail stores for food. The maximum monthly food stamp allotment for a family of four is $209, equal to the Department of Agriculture's Thrifty Food Plan of 59 cents per meal for each person. This amount

Figure 13 Food stamp program expansion

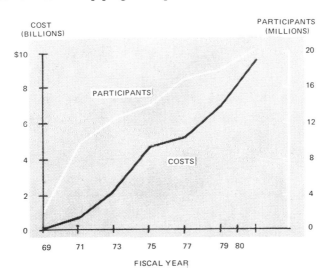

SOURCE: U.S. Department of Agriculture

is reduced by 30 percent of a household's net income (after certain allowable deductions) based on the assumption, similar to that used in calculating the poverty threshold, that a family spends one-third of its income on food. This allows a family of four with a monthly income of $500 to receive $82 in food stamps per month ($209 less 30 percent of $500 minus a $75 standard deduction). Benefit levels are adjusted periodically to reflect changes in food prices.

Since its reinstitution in 1961, the food stamp program has been jointly operated by both the federal and state governments and is available in all states. The federal government finances the direct cost of food stamps and a share of state program administrative costs. The responsibility for program administration and the distribution of food stamps is left to each state.

After a slow start in the 1960s, the program grew rapidly during the 1970s. The expansion of food stamps in the 1970s paralleled the growth of cash welfare in the late 1960s. Among the important factors were:

79

1. The wider availability of benefits. About 60 percent of the population in 1969 lived in areas served by the program; by 1975 all of the population had access to food stamp benefits as the commodity distribution program was phased out.

2. More generous benefits. Congress enacted generally higher benefits and removed obstacles to participation for the poorest families. In addition, benefits are to be adjusted semiannually by the increase in the cost of living.

3. Increased utilization. An increasing proportion of public assistance households, who are automatically eligible, availed itself of benefits as a result of extensive media publicity and the outreach efforts of public and private groups.

4. Higher unemployment during the 1970s. The Agriculture Department estimated that each 1 percent rise in the unemployment rate might add about 600,000 additional participants.

A purported reason cited by the program's critics was fraud. Although there were many errors in determining eligibility and computing benefits, these errors had a limited effect on the overall number of recipients, and charges of widespread fraud were not substantiated. In spite of the extensive and rapid growth, it was estimated that by 1980 three in ten eligible persons were still not receiving food stamps.

In an attempt to restrict food stamps to only those who could not support themselves, Congress established a work requirement. Except for persons with child-care responsibilities, students, and persons already working, all able-bodied persons between 18 and 65 in households receiving food stamps must register for employment and accept suitable work paying the going rate in the locality even though it may be below the federal minimum in some cases.

Concerned by the increase in beneficiaries and potential further expansion, Congress in 1977 passed the Food Stamp Act aimed at reducing benefit levels for the near-poor while increasing levels of support for the more needy. Eligibility was narrowed from individuals with incomes not more than 125 percent of the poverty level to those whose incomes were 100 percent of the poverty level or less. Allowable income deductions used in determining eligibility were also reduced and the rate at which benefits are reduced in response to increases in income was increased. In order to create greater accessibility to food assistance for the very poor, the 1977 legislation eliminated the "cash purchase" requirement which provided that food stamps had to be bought by recipients at a cost that varied by income and made it difficult for many poor families to participate in the program. The net effect of these changes was to remove an estimated 1 million individuals from the rolls, substantially reduce benefits for as many as 3 million more, and induce an additional 3 million persons to enter the program by 1979. Several other attempts were made to contain burgeoning program costs. The 1977 act placed an aggregate ceiling on the food stamp budget of $6.2 billion for fiscal years 1979 to 1981. This was subsequently changed in 1980 to $8.75 billion as inflation diminished the purchasing power of a household's food dollars. The 1979 Food Stamp Act took another approach to containing costs by tightening regulations in an effort to cut down on incidences of fraud, abuse, and waste. Among other provisions, incentives were provided for states to verify recipients' income, and all recipients were required to furnish social security numbers to facilitate this process. Legislation pending in 1980 would add additional provisions against fraud, such as increasing the federal share of costs for investigation of abuses and computerization of recipient data, in attempts to find ways to keep expenditures from rising. It is also being proposed to calculate school lunch benefits into a family's net income and to adjust benefit levels once a year. In mid-1980, with rising food costs and threatening rising levels of unemployment, it is doubtful that more recent efforts to contain the costs of the food stamp program will be more successful in the immediate future than the cap on spending legislated three years earlier.

All public assistance recipients are eligible to receive food stamps except SSI recipients in states that provide food stamp benefits in the form of increased SSI payments. Only households with net incomes at or below the poverty level, after certain allowable deductions are subtracted, are eligible. In 1978 close to 90 percent of all food stamp recipients had gross incomes (before any deductions) below the poverty level. Over half of the recipients also received public assistance, 22 percent were SSI recipients, and 21 percent were receiving social security income.

The program has been successful in targeting benefits to those most in need and in offering assistance to the working poor. According to the Agriculture Department, two out of every three food stamp households are headed by a woman, more than one in four family heads are 55 years or older, and over half of all participants are 18 years or younger. In 1978, over half of participating households had an income of less than $3,600, and another 21 percent had incomes between $3,600 and $4,800. Less than 12 percent of family heads receiving food stamp benefits were employed full time.

Still some families who would not normally be considered poor were able to participate—nearly 3 percent of all recipients in 1978 had an income of $9,000 or more—because various costs were deducted from a family's gross income to compute eligibility and benefit amount. In addition to a $75 standard deduction, allowance is also made for a deduction of 20 percent of earned income (to make up for work-related expenses and social security and income taxes), as well as child care and extra high housing costs. Though it is not common, a family of four with a gross annual income of $11,412 could be eligible to receive $30 in monthly food stamps by deducting a possible $355 a month, leaving a net income for food stamp purposes of $596 a month. The average monthly deduction claimed by 84 percent of food stamp families in 1978 was $197.

Although recipients would undoubtedly find cash easier and less demeaning to use, food stamps may be used to purchase any food for human consumption except alcoholic beverages, tobacco, and imported food (no Russian caviar). Aside from the fact that food stamps cannot be used for housecleaning and laundry supplies, medicines, and many other items carried in supermarkets, there are other operational limitations. Nor are benefits adequate. The food stamp bonus is supposed to enable a family to maintain what the Department of Agriculture calls a "nutritionally adequate" diet, but this regimen requires nutritional planning skills, storage space, equipment, and low-cost markets.

Yet the importance of the food stamp program in the scope of federal antipoverty efforts is beyond dispute. Even while the program fails to meet the complete nutritional needs of recipients, it has improved the access of the poor to essential food supplies. Perhaps more importantly, the food stamp program remains one of the few federal initiatives that extend to the working poor, and in so doing it preserves some sense of equity for that neglected segment of the American population.

Child Nutrition

Aside from the broad effort to use food stamps as a vehicle for aid to the American poor, federal food assistance has been sharply focused on the area of child nutrition. A variety of programs now provide breakfast, lunch, and milk to children in private and public schools and day care centers, at a total federal cost in 1980 of about $3.9 billion. Federal aid is provided through state agencies in the form of cash or commodities that subsidize nutritional meals for children, with special aid targeted at children from low-income families.

By far the largest is the school lunch program, with federal costs in fiscal 1979 of $1.7 billion. Nearly 25 million children, about five in nine, received lunch daily. Federal reimbursement is provided on the basis of all meals served, regardless of children's family income, and additional assistance is provided for meals served free or at reduced cost to children from poor or near-poor families. In 1979 about 9.9 million children from poor or near-poor homes received free meals at an average federal subsidy of 93 cents per meal, 1.7 million received reduced-price lunches at an average subsidy of 73 cents, and 13 million children received lunches at an average federal cost of 17 cents.

The school breakfast and special milk programs are smaller in scope, and yet still have a significant impact on child nutrition. Free or reduced-priced breakfasts were offered to over 3 million children in fiscal year 1979, with a maximum subsidy of about 57 cents per meal and at a total federal cost of over $207 million. Similarly, the special milk program provided added nourishment to nearly 2 million children in participating schools, institutions, and summer camps at a federal cost of $126 million.

Child nutrition programs reach outside of the traditional school setting to provide in-kind aid in summer camps, day care centers, and local health clinics. Over 500,000 children, mostly from poor homes, received these meals. Finally, the special supplemental feeding program for women, infants, and children channels aid to local health clinics serving low-income areas, with an average of 1.6 million persons participating and an estimated cost in 1979 of $550 million.

Despite the significant progress, some serious flaws remain in the school lunch program, especially in serving the poor. For every two children who received free or reduced-price lunches, at least one more child, perhaps several million altogether, was eligible but did not benefit. The process of establishing eligibility can be complicated for the applicant and can create a great deal of paper work for the schools. Moreover, children who qualify for free or reduced-price lunches are often singled out by standing in separate lines, eating at specified tables, or using distinctive lunch tokens. The involved certification procedures and stigmatization of children may discourage many needy children from applying for free meals. Many more children are denied this opportunity because their school does not have the necessary equipment or funds to meet federal matching requirements for operating expenses. This is especially true of schools in poor neighborhoods. Thus, those children who most need the nutritional benefits of a school lunch are also those most likely to go to schools without such programs. While the advances brought by child nutrition programs since the mid-1960s are significant, their shortcomings underscore the special barriers that can accompany programs of indirect, in-kind assistance to the poor.

Social Services

As federal programs for the poor expanded during the 1960s, Congress increasingly acknowledged the importance of social services in helping the poor cope with their own lives and preserving some stability for future generations. While the scope of social services is so broad as to defy definition, they range from specifics, such as child and foster care, family planning, drug and alcohol abuse treatment, and legal aid, to more vague forms of assistance, such as counseling or strengthening family life. Services to the mentally retarded and support programs for the elderly are also included in the gamut of services offered. The mere process of determining whether someone has a problem, even if nothing can be done to relieve it, is regarded as a social service.

Yet if the content of social services is somewhat amorphous, the cost certainly is not. Under a 1967 law authorizing open-ended federal matching funds (three federal dollars for every state dollar) for service to former, current, or potential welfare recipients, state requests for federal funds quickly ballooned to over $4 billion by

1972. The congressional response to burgeoning program costs set a precedent later applied to the food stamp program—an annual ceiling on federal expenditures limited outlays for this purpose to $2.5 billion. While subsequent congresses had slowly raised this spending cap to $2.9 billion by 1979, the ceiling has successfully held social service costs well below growth rates in other federal in-kind assistance programs.

Because federal social service programs do not have the large and established constituencies of federal health care, housing, or food stamp programs, there have been few efforts to expand federal responsibilities markedly in this area, and most program reforms have been designed to narrow the focus and scope of services to the poor. In 1974, Congress targeted social service expenditures to more specific goals and directed that at least half of expenditures be used to aid public assistance recipients. The 1974 law also restricted free services to families whose income was below either the national median or 80 percent of the state median income. Other congressional initiatives emphasized family planning services for the poor by raising the federal matching grants for this purpose from 75 to 90 percent, and more recently targeted special aid at child care services and child welfare services designed to keep low-income families together and enable adults in the family to work. While such efforts can be viewed as long-range investments and alternatives to costly cash and in-kind assistance programs, the federal commitment to social services is certain to lag far behind the massive outlays for the daily necessities of the poor in the coming decade.

Changing Institutions

In virtually all federal in-kind assistance programs—medical services, shelter, food, and social services—the pattern of development throughout the 1960s and 1970s was strikingly uniform. The federal government in all these programs responded to the relatively immediate needs of the poor, demonstrated a consistent preference for in-kind rather than cash aid, and ultimately searched for ways to control costs as federal outlays reached ever-increasing levels. Yet in one unique federal initiative—community action—the goals and the philosophy have been markedly different. In struggling with its distinctive role in federal antipoverty efforts, the community action approach has carved a history all its own.

Arising out of President Johnson's War on Poverty in the mid-1960s, the community action experiment tested a bold, unprecedented approach to the problems of the poor. Rather than responding to the immediate needs of Americans in poverty, or even to the long-range personal barriers (for example, lack of education and training and the need for family planning) to individual advancement, community action embraced the ambitious goal of structural and institutional changes attempting to alter some of the fundamental social, political, and economic forces that trapped the poor in poverty. Unlike other federal programs in aid of the poor, the goal of community action was not simply to raise the effective income of the poor, it was to change the very equation by which millions of Americans inevitably found themselves below the poverty threshold each year.

The structure of community action efforts was carefully drafted in response to the lessons of more traditional antipoverty programs. The architects of the Great Society recognized that the insulated federal bureaucracy was far removed from the needs and realities of the populations it served, and that the tradition of grudging and paternal assistance contributed little to individual self-esteem or to the collective abilities of the poor. As an alternative, the Johnson administration sought a strategy for fighting poverty that required the participation of the poor in the design and operation of the programs that served them. By attempting to involve the poor in the decision-making process, including the choice of services and delivery systems, the intent was to promote as much discretion and innovation as possible at the local level. Ultimately, three primary vehicles for this new approach emerged: the Community Action Program (CAP), legal services, and the community development corporations.

A product of the Great Society's Economic Opportunity Act of 1964, CAP funded the establishment of almost 1,000 local community action agencies (CAAs) in urban neighborhoods, in rural areas, and on Indian reservations. The poor were represented on their planning boards and in many cases were hired to help operate the programs. The CAAs quickly became a catchall for projects aiding the poor, acting as sponsors for a variety of social programs funded by federal, state, local, and private agencies. While practically any effort aimed at reducing poverty may be funded through CAAs, the long-run CAP strategy remains focused on the mobilization of nonfederal resources to respond to local needs and the development of mechanisms through which the poor can make their needs known to local government officials, civic organizations, employers, and labor interests who are in a position to offer direct local assistance.

In creating a program designed to alter the very institutions and political structure on which it depended for its existence, the Community Action Program created some internal tensions that it could withstand only temporarily. The 1967 amendments to the Economic Opportunity Act began to undermine the basic CAP strategy by seeking to bring more CAAs under public control, and while only 140 (about half on Indian reservations) were public by 1973, the pendulum had clearly started to swing back toward programs under the political control of local public officials. The Nixon administration asserted this approach forcefully at the start of its second term, dismantling in 1974 the Office of Economic Opportunity, which was both the symbol and the driving force of community action. Employment and training programs were shifted to the domain of designated elected officials rather than CAAs under the Comprehensive Employment and Training Act of 1973, and the model cities program was consolidated into community development block grants controlled by local officials under the Housing and Community Development Act of 1974. The Congress did salvage the community action program by transferring it to a newly created Community Services Administration in HEW, but the mandate for institutional change in the broadest sense had disappeared.

In more recent years, the CAAs and related community-based organizations have continued working, even if with a lower profile, in federal antipoverty efforts. They have maintained an active role in employment and training programs for both youth and adults, and continue to sponsor Head Start and other specialized education programs. More importantly, the Congress reversed a trend of declining federal support for the CAAs, agreeing in 1978 to extend CAAs to rural areas and to raise the federal/local matching requirement to 80/20 (the federal share of CAA support had fallen from 90 percent to 60 percent between 1964 and 1977). It would be a mistake to view the current activities of the CAAs as fulfilling the promise of the community action philosophy of 1964, for in most communities they have neither the power nor in some cases the will to mobilize the poor. Yet the CAAs certainly continue to serve as a vehicle for conveying the needs of the poor to less sensitive institutions while offering a broad range of services more consistent with traditional approaches to federal antipoverty programs.

Closely related to the CAAs is VISTA (Volunteers in Service to America), also established by the 1964 antipoverty law to enlist volunteers for the antipoverty effort. Although VISTA merged with other volunteer efforts to form the ACTION program in 1971, a large percentage of the agency volunteers remain active on CAA-sponsored projects. Their work varies from legal aid to community development to disaster relief. In addition to the regular VISTA volunteers who contributed approximately 3,700 years of service during 1979, some 800 students also devoted a year's work in exchange for academic credit as part of the University Year for Action program. In recent years, VISTA has been forced to weather attacks on community action activities and attempts to dismantle the parent ACTION agency. However, the concept of volunteerism has shielded the VISTA program from most efforts to restrict activist work representing and organizing the poor.

As the second primary vehicle of the community action initiative, the antipoverty legal services program was the most controversial and perhaps the most significant experiment of the Economic Opportunity Act of 1964. As the interface between the poor and the institutions that community action sought to change, the law was a natural starting point in attempts to intervene on behalf of the poor. Whether in land-lord-tenant problems, wage garnishments for unpaid debts, excessive interest charges and shoddy workmanship by ghetto merchants, or conflicts with police and juvenile authorities, the poor are the most likely to confront the law and the least prepared to cope with the system. Organized legal aid societies have long provided some services to the poor, but the legal services program of the Office of Economic Opportunity was the first federal effort to improve the distribution of legal aid and to bolster the odds of the poor in the legal system.

Most of the cases undertaken by legal services projects were fairly standard matters. More than one-third of the cases involved family disputes, such as divorce, nonsupport, and custody of children; three in ten consumer or housing problems; and one in ten noncriminal adult and juvenile proceedings. Of the remaining cases, two of every three concerned administrative disputes or decisions by government bureaucracies that affect the poor. Although few in number, these cases attracted the greatest public attention and controversy. In this category legal services may have made the more lasting mark. Among the most far-reaching cases eventually decided by the Supreme Court were those that opened the public assistance rolls to more needy persons.

In its brief but stormy history, the legal services program in OEO made friends among the poor and disenfranchised but also many enemies in the established power bases. As the effort to dismantle OEO reached its peak in 1973, several years of harsh criticism focusing on the legal services program also culminated in the transfer of legal aid efforts to an independent Legal Services Corporation. The 1974 legislation creating the corporation included a wide range of restrictions on the agency and its attorneys, including bans on representation in cases concerning school desegregation, nontherapeutic abortions, and certain criminal cases. Later amendments to the Legal Services Corporation Act lifed a variety of other restrictions originally passed in 1974, including bans on policital activity (partisan or otherwise), representation of juveniles, and the use of corporation funds for research, training, and technical assistance related to the delivery of legal services. The vast majority of cases now handled by the Legal Services Corporation are similar in nature to those confronted in the legal services program of OEO, but some of the freedom and autonomy to pursue legal issues of importance to the poor have undoubtedly been lost.

The third vehicle for community action adopted by the Great Society policymakers experimented with a radical approach to solving some of the fundamental, chronic problems that contribute to poverty. Community Development Corporations (CDCs) were the first sustained effort at building a solid economic base in poor communities. On the federal level these corporations received funding and commitments for support from the Office of Economic Opportunity, the Small Business Administration, and the Department of Housing and Urban Development. At the local level the corporations received enthusiastic moral support from many politicians and community activists and, to a lesser extent, further financial support.

The CDCs were established to support a variety of community-based enterprises that included manufacturing firms, service ventures, retail establishments, and construction firms. Having failed to create a self-sustaining economic base in poor communities, the Nixon administration shifted away from a reliance on CDCs in the early 1970s, and chose alternative mechanisms such as the Minority Enterprise Small Business Investment Company (MESBIC) and the targeting of loans through the Small Business Administration (SBA). In retrospect, there is little reason to believe that minority enterprises under MESBIC and SBA programs fared any better than the CDCs. To the extent that the benefits of the CDCs were not limited to the narrow realm of economic development, the shift in emphasis to minority enterprises in isolation falls far short of the community action role envisioned in the original CDC program.

In the 1980s, many Americans believe that the community action programs of the War on Poverty died with the Office of Economic Opportunity years ago. Nothing could be farther from the truth. Some community action agencies are alive and reasonably well, albeit in modified form in comparison to the hopes envisioned for them by the Great Society antipoverty warriors. The most aggressive elements of the community action concept are gone, frequently coopted by the very institutions and power structures they were designed to challenge on behalf of the poor. Yet there remains a stong and active strain of community participation and of greater awareness of the needs of the poor, as the community action agencies continue to attempt to organize the poor and to provide a wide range of essential services on their behalf.

The Overlap of Cash and In-Kind Aid

The overlap of cash and in-kind assistance is inevitable, and, in many cases, desirable. The most obvious—and intended—result is an increase in the ecomomic well-being of recipients. Virtually all public assistance recipients receive medical benefits, 78 percent get food stamps, and about one in four lives in subsidized housing. Some families on public assistance receive none of this in-kind assistance, while others may benefit from several programs. Three-quarters of Old Age, Survivors, and Disability Insurance recipients are helped by Medicare. Even these limited data show considerable overlap, and complete information would presumably show much more.

Some proponents of in-kind assistance hope that the needy would benefit from as many programs as they qualify for. But there are very serious problems not only in coordinating eligibility for these benefits but in adjusting the level of these benefits as outside earnings change. The present arrangement of administering most of these programs separately exacerbates this problem.

The disincentives have a devastating effect on AFDC families, who are the ones most likely to be able to supplement their assistance with earnings and are also most likely to benefit from one or more in-kind programs. As an AFDC family's earnings rise, it is confronted first of all with a decrease in its assistance payment (losing 67 cents in aid for each dollar earned after the first $30 and work expenses), a social security tax of 6.13 percent on all covered earnings, and a federal income tax of at least 13 percent on earnings above $8,600 for a family of four. In net cash income alone, an AFDC family receives limited rewards for working.

If the family also receives food stamps, the incentives to work are further diminished. In addition, a most perverse problem arises from Medicaid. The program covers *all* of a beneficiary's medical expenses or none. When a family is no longer eligible, all benefits cease. A family of four that receives the average benefit of $1,480 each year may lose all of this assistance by earning an extra $100. Families who also receive school lunches and public housing are confronted with an even more difficult choice.

The cumulative decrease in benefits as income rises—the cumulative tax rate—is illustrated in table 4. Maintaining meaningful work incentives for a family receiving several forms of aid is one of the thorniest problems in welfare reform.

Given the multiplicity of income support and in-kind programs and the diversity of eligibility rules and certification procedures, there is room for persons to exploit the system and, no doubt, some have. A tendency exists, however, to exaggerate the inequities resulting from duplication. For example, a General Accounting Office study found that participation in multiple programs was largely a function of

Table 4. Benefits potentially available to a female-headed family of four, 1979

| Earnings | AFDC[1] | Taxes | | Earned Income Tax Credit | Net Cash | Food Stamps[2] | Net Cash and Food Stamps | Medicaid[3] |
		Social Security	Income					
—	$3,600	—	—	—	$3,600	$1,698	$5,298	$1480
$ 1,000	3,573	$ 61	—	98	4,610	1,466	6,076	1480
2,000	2,903	123	—	198	4,978	1,427	6,405	1480
3,000	2,233	184	—	298	5,347	1,388	6,735	1480
4,000	1,563	245	—	398	5,716	1,349	7,065	1480
5,000	893	307	—	498	6,084	1,310	7,394	1480
6,000	223	368	—	500	6,365	1,271	7,636	1480
7,000	—	429	95	378	6,854	1,098	7,952	—
8,000	—	490	235	253	7,528	858	8,386	—
9,000	—	552	394	128	8,182	618	8,800	—
10,000	—	613	546	—	8,841	378	9,219	—

[1] Assumes the state pays $300 per month and uses the standard "$30 and one-third" formula, and that the family has work expenses of $50 a month.
[2] Assumes a $75 standard deduction and a 20 percent work expense deduction on total earned income.
[3] Based on average benefit received by Medicaid recipients times the average number of persons in AFDC households in May 1979.

family size—large families face multiple needs and tend, therefore, to participate in more programs. It is doubtful whether a single cash assistance program could provide for all these needs.

ADDITIONAL READINGS

Fuchs, Victor R. *Who Shall Live.* New York: Basic Books, 1975.
Kamerman, Sheila B., and Kahn, Alfred J.' *Social Services in the United States: Policies and Programs.* Philadelphia: Temple University Press, 1976.
Levin, Arthur, ed. *Health Service.* New York: Academy of Political Science, 1977.
Levitan, Sar A. *The Great Society's Poor Law.* Baltimore: Johns Hopkins University Press, 1969.
Lewis, Charles E.; Fein, Rashi; and Mechanic, David. *A Right to Health.* New York: John Wiley & Sons, 1976.
U.S. Congressional Budget Office. *Food Stamp Program.* Washington, D.C.: Government Printing Office, 1979.
U.S. Congressional Budget Office. *The Long-Term Costs of Lower-Income Housing Assistance Programs.* Washington, D.C.: Government Printing Office, 1979.

DISCUSSION QUESTIONS

1. "It is undesirable to provide poor families with food, housing, medical care, and other 'in-kind' payments at cut-rate prices. When subsidies are desirable, the government should provide cash subsidies and allow people to spend it as they wish." Discuss.

2. Some have argued that in order to estimate the number of poor people, it is necessary to include the value of the in-kind income they receive. What are the technical difficulties in costing out in-kind goods and services?

3. Why has in-kind aid to the poor in the 1970s grown more rapidly than cash assistance?

4. What are the pro and con arguments to providing the poor only cash assistance?

5. Consider the factors that have contributed to the rapid increases in providing health care for the poor.

6. What have been the criticisms of public housing and what strategies has the Great Society favored to provide subsidized shelter for the poor?

7. Discuss the pros and cons of providing food stamps as contrasted with cash assistance.

8. How do the goals of community action agencies differ from the objectives of providing social services for the poor?

9. What combination of in-kind and cash aid would you favor to help the poor?

10. How did the philosophy underlying the Community Action Program differ from the provision of social services?

11. A significant phenomenon of recent years has been the increasing overlap between the wage structure and the benefits available from public assistance programs. What are the reasons for this development? What do you see as the consequences? Appraise the political prospects and potential effectiveness of proposals designed to deal with this phenomenon.

4

Programs for the Next Generation

Train up a child in the way he should go; and when he is old, he will not depart from it.

—Proverbs 22:6

The experience of the past two decades—especially the ever-increasing costs of programs and services for the poor—offers some sobering lessons for federal policy. Under the Great Society of the 1960s, antipoverty programs were advocated with an optimistic view of the potential of federal efforts in aid of the poor, believing that a major commitment could eradicate poverty in our lifetime. The events of the 1970s suggested that it is a much more difficult and expensive endeavor. Not only have the poor remained, but the nation has shown a reluctance to provide the level of support necessary to meet even the most basic needs of Americans below the poverty level.

There is no question that the immediate needs of the poor—income, food, shelter, health care—continue to place the most pressing demands on government funds for the poor. Yet the costs of this effort are a constant reminder of the importance of steps to reduce the ranks of the poor in the future. Funds for the prevention of poverty may not show definite, positive results for many years, but they are still the cornerstone of help in an affluent society.

The obvious focus of prevention efforts is the next generation, the children of the poor. The federal role in attempting to shield the next generation from poverty has centered on three major areas: birth control, child care, and education. Assisting couples in keeping family size within their desires and means will aid the next generation to begin at less of a disadvantage. Providing care to preschool children can alleviate the pressures of poverty that bring the neglect of physical and social development during crucial formative years. Investing in the education of the next generation will better equip the children of the poor to compete in the job market and to find alternatives to dependency.

The heavy reliance on the direct provision of services to the next generation—as opposed to additional cash assistance to the poor for these purposes—is hardly coincidental. In some cases, the in-kind approach is the only way to ensure effective aid; for example, cash assistance to cover birth control information or devices would probably not increase their use by the poor. Birth control devices must be widely distributed, easily available, highly publicized, and *used* if they are to be effective. Other services, such as education, are more efficiently provided by the government because of economies of scale, and, therefore, direct provision is necessary.

BIRTH CONTROL

The close relationship between large families, unwanted births, and poverty is well documented. As the number of youngsters in a household increases so does the probability that the family will be destitute (see figure 3). Data support the adage that "the rich get richer and the poor get children." But medical technology is now available to control household size and therefore alleviate one of the conditions that has often caused poverty.

The deprivation of many families could have been prevented if practical means for birth control had been provided. Contrary to widely held misconceptions that the poor have more children because they want them, a longitudinal survey of about 5,000 American families conducted by the University of Michigan's Survey Research Center indicates that economic status and race have little bearing on the desired family size. All wanted approximately the same number of children but the poor got more, or they had added mouths to feed that made them poor.

Not only has there been a marked increase in the number of adults who use some form of birth control, but the methods employed have changed as more people use contraceptives. Beyond sheer numbers, the quality of birth control methods used has also improved.

Besides scientific advances, the laws associated with birth control have changed. The most significant change was represented by a 1973 Supreme Court decision that struck down restrictive state laws regarding abortion, especially during the first three months of pregnancy. At the same time national opinion research indicates vast changes in attitudes toward abortion. In 1968 about seven out of eight adults were against abortion when the only reason would be the desire not to have another child. The proportion of people who feel this way had fallen to about one-half by 1978. Back in 1959 about 73 percent of adult Americans surveyed believed that birth control information should be available to anyone who wants it. By 1977 this percentage had risen to over 91 percent. The largest change has been in the attitudes expressed by Catholics. In 1964 only three out of five Catholics favored the distribution of birth control information, but by 1977, six out of seven Catholics favored this position.

The changes in bedroom technology and law notwithstanding, unwanted and unplanned births are still significant factors in American society. The incidence of unwanted births is greater for the lower-income and poorly educated population. The University of Michigan survey found that destitute families have about a one-third chance of an unwanted baby. For households earning about twice the poverty level or more, this probability falls to under 25 percent. A woman with a college degree has only about an 8 percent chance that she will have an unwanted birth, but for women who have less than a high school diploma this chance increases to roughly 33 percent. The evidence is clear that limited access to birth control devices and family planning services has prevented many women unable to afford medical care from exercising the same degree of choice as more affluent women.

In 1978, one of every seven births in the United States was without the blessing of church and state. The percentage of all children born out of wedlock has risen sharply, and in the last two decades it more than doubled. Half of all black births and about one of every twelve white births are out of wedlock.

There have been some declines in the illegitimacy rates for women 20 years and older. This is due to a wider acceptance and availability of family planning methods. However, these benefits have not filtered down to many teenage women who are the mothers of more than half the children born out of wedlock. Limited knowledge and use of contraceptive devices as well as restricted accessibility have kept illegitimate births by teenage mothers at their high level.

About 10 percent of all females between the ages of 15 and 19 become pregnant annually, accounting for close to 600,000 births per year. Of this total, more than three of seven are born out of wedlock. In almost nine of ten cases, the teenage mother decides to keep the child; 8 percent are put up for adoption while the rest are sent to live with other relatives. Black teenage mothers on average show a higher propensity to keep their children born out of wedlock than white teenagers.

There is ample evidence that a teenage single mother is going to face all sorts of problems that are likely to have lasting effects; her education is likely to be interrupted and the child may present insurmountable impediments to securing a job. In many such cases, both mother and child end up on welfare. According to the latest survey of Aid to Families with Dependent Children, teenagers account for more than a quarter-million AFDC mothers. Even if the parents do marry and support their offspring, their education is still likely to be interrupted and their job opportunities may be limited for life. There is also considerable evidence that early parenthood leads to larger families, placing continuing economic burdens upon the household.

Programs designed to increase the knowledge and availability of birth control for young woman could have a major impact in reducing poverty. About two-thirds of all teenage pregnancies are not intentional. There does appear to be a strong relationship between out-of-wedlock birth rates and the availability of legal abortion. In the early 1970s the greatest declines in out-of-wedlock birthrates occurred in states that had liberal abortion laws.

The reduction of birthrates among the poor would have many positive effects. Fewer children would be born into poor households, and fewer households would be driven into poverty because of unwanted children. This would help keep people out of poverty and would arrest the acceleration of relief costs.

Lower welfare costs are only a part of the total savings that accrue from birth control programs, just as AFDC payments are only one of the many costs of poverty. Nor are dollar savings the major reason for providing assistance to prevent the birth of unwanted children. The primary goal is the reduction of human misery. Birth control services can, for example, substantially improve health among the poor. Physical examinations for low-income women will help in detecting cervical cancer and other diseases. Having too many children too close together is a major contributor to infant mortality, mental retardation, physical defects, and premature births. Frequent pregnancy is recognized as a health hazard to the mother as well, draining her energy and contributing to high maternal death rates. The Department of Health and Human Services has confirmed that fertility control is the most effective means of reducing infant death rates and improving maternal and infant health. An additional benefit of fertility control is that children in smaller families tend to receive better care and are less likely candidates for a life of poverty than children in larger families.

It is estimated that about 6.5 million poor and near-poor women were in need of organized family planning services in 1980. The cost of providing a patient with a medical examination and birth control devices is about $90 a year. A comprehensive program to furnish services would cost under $600 million annually. While total funding for family planning services rose dramatically during the late 1960s and 1970s, the allocation of resources to this area has been way under the potential demand. In 1980 the federal government spent $165 million on family planning services compared to only $16 million in 1968 (excluding payments for services provided by private physicians). In addition, outlays for population and contraception research increased from $8.4 million to $86 million in the same time span. The outlays by state and local governments and private organizations are not available.

American society has undergone dramatic shifts in opinion regarding both birth control and government activity in promoting family planning programs. Despite these changes in social views, family planning and abortion have remained hot political topics. Efforts to block government funding of some abortions have been seriously considered in both Congress and the courts.

However, the increasing support of federal legislation with the goal of providing family planning services to all indigent women who need and desire them reflects an expanded consensus that fertility control is not only a valuable contribution to family life but also an effective measure of preventing poverty. The origins of federal family planning policies began with Title V of the 1935 Social Security Act. It established formula grants to states for maternal and child health, of which family planning was a component. Congress demonstrated its increased support of the concept in 1967 by earmarking up to 6 percent of Title V funds for family planning and by requiring that birth control services be offered to AFDC mothers under Medicaid.

Under the Family Planning Services and Population Research Act of 1970, low-income persons are to be given priority, but services are not restricted to the poor. A 1978 amendment provided that 6 percent of the family planning funds be earmarked for services to teenagers. The goal is to expand services in areas with high teenage birth rates.

In 1972 Congress made coverage of family planning services mandatory under Medicaid. The federal contribution makes up 90 percent of the outlays in this area. The number of women served by organized programs rose from under 1 million in 1968 to more than 4.3 million a decade later (figure 14). Roughly three out of every four clients had incomes of less than 150 percent of the poverty level. An additional 1.6 million low-income women received family planning services from private physicians. Despite the rapid expansion of federal family planning services, an estimated 29 percent of eligible low-income women of childbearing age received no subsidized family planning services in 1978. Public assistance recipients made up one-fifth of the women served by ongoing programs and accounted for about one-fourth of eligible women assisted by public welfare.

CHILD CARE

The impact of poverty on children can be lasting, and its imprint of deprivation lies at the very root of intergenerational poverty. The home environment has a fundamental influence on the development of children, and the offspring of the poor often grow up without the benefit of the many forms of support—emotional, social, intellectual,

Figure 14 Number of patients receiving family planning services

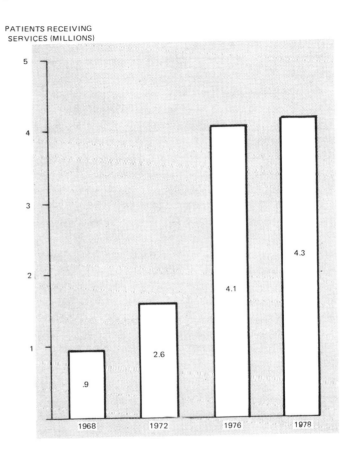

SOURCE: Alan Guttmacher Institute

and financial—that would move them closer to the realization of their full potential.

Previous chapters have already touched upon some of the federal programs that address the most basic needs of poor children, including medical services and child nutrition efforts. With the

101

proportion of preschool children whose mothers worked or looked for work rising and the efforts to induce poor women with children to enter the work force, federal outlays for child care programs have grown rapidly since the Great Society focused on the special needs of poor children.

Institutions outside the home are playing an increasingly important role in socializing and educating children and adolescents. However, the home environment still has a fundamental influence on the young, and poverty can seriously and permanently impair their ability to realize educational opportunities. Impoverished children often experience great difficulties during their school years, not only because of health deficiencies and inadequate diet but also because they lack verbal and sensory stimulation in their family environment. Older youths face difficulties in high school and may drop out of school because their motivation and resources are limited. Children from poor families must have special attention from the very start if they are to succeed in school.

Most local institutions are unable or unwilling to offer this assistance. In poor neighborhoods, where schools are typically deficient in resources, facilities, and personnel, the federal government has developed a variety of supportive services to help children from impoverished homes mature into independent adulthood. Such services range from assistance for day care of preschool children to financial support for indigent youths in college.

Child and Maternal Care

Children's aid programs were the first social welfare services provided by the federal government, dating back to the Taft administration. While child and maternal services are not aimed exclusively at children of poor families, most beneficiaries are from low-income families. A government brochure describing the child welfare services, for example, announces that the program is designed "for troubled children and children in trouble." Problems of child neglect, abuse, and emotional disturbance are not found exclusively in indigent homes, but it is hardly surprising that poor children have more than their share of such problems. Consequently, children from impoverished homes are likely candidates for assistance offered by child welfare programs.

Even with this long history of child welfare services offered without regard to economic status, the major federal commitment to child care services for the poor has emerged only recently. The 1967 amendments to the Social Security Act took the first significant step in this regard, consolidating health services for mothers, infants, preschool and school children, and crippled children as well as authorizing grants to states for preventive health care and for research in these areas. With the creation of the Office of Child Development in 1969 (now under the Department of Health and Human Services), Congress more formally acknowledged a federal role in child advocacy and development through day care and other child welfare services. Building upon this foundation, the 1970s became in some sense the "decade of the child" as the federal government broadly embraced the concept of child care as a major responsibility in meeting the needs of the next generation.

The principal source of direct federal support for general child care services is the state-administered social services program under Title XX of the Social Security Act. In 1980, states used nearly $600 million in federal funds for various kinds of child care service to low- and middle-income families, with the greatest portion funneled to day care centers. While the federal matching requirement for social services is generally 75 percent, the Congress has emphasized its commitment to child care by earmarking $200 million annually since 1977 for this purpose at 100 percent federal matching. Representing over one-fifth of all federal social services outlays under Title XX, this support for child care shows no sign of waning in the 1980s.

A further boost to federal involvement in child care developed as a by-product of the creation of the Work Incentive (WIN) program, established in 1967 to place "appropriate" adult AFDC recipients in training programs and jobs as alternatives to welfare dependency. In order to enable AFDC mothers to participate in the program and to take on jobs, the legislation requires states to provide child care arrangements for women enrolled in the program. Formal facilities involving large numbers of children and in-home arrangements must meet standards developed by the state. The federal government provides 90 percent of the financing. Day care or child development facilities can also be provided as a social service under Aid to Families with Dependent Children. States may set up facilities in poor neighborhoods and provide day care to any child supported by AFDC.

103

The complete list of federal programs offering support for child care services encompasses a broad range of legislative initiatives, including the community development program administered by HUD, the community action agency programs funded by the Community Services Administration, the employment and training programs run by the Department of Labor, state child welfare programs assisted by the Department of Health and Human Services, and more limited efforts funded through the Appalachian Regional Commission and the Bureau of Indian Affairs.

In addition, the largest federal subsidies for child care are provided through indirect tax expenditures, including an estimated $700 million in federal tax credits for child care expenses in 1980 and nearly $85 million in added AFDC benefits as a result of the deduction of child care expenses from gross income in 1977. While less visible, these mechanisms for indirect support of child care have a dramatic impact on the ability of parents to afford appropriate day care and other child welfare services. These programs may also address themselves to the child's health and general development.

The rising outlays for child care in the 1970s were accompanied by a federal debate regarding the appropriate content of child care services and the need for federal standards governing the provision of such services. Certainly there are risks in the delivery of child care services. At worst, child care can be merely shuffling children from one destitute household to another while depriving them of the personal attention that they might receive from their own families. At best, it can offer opportunities for learning, socializing, and individual care by professional staff that surpasses the potential of the home environment, but the cost of this type of comprehensive care runs extremely high. In recent years, the concept of federal staffing requirements for day care services has been the focal point of intense controversy—generous federal standards were developed as early as 1968 but proved impractical to enforce on federally-supported child care projects because the requirements would have raised costs dramatically and would have reduced the ability of public and private agencies to serve low-income families. With the number of "slots" in state-licensed day care centers and homes equaling less than one-fourth the total number of children under age six with mothers in the labor force, even substandard care may prove more valuable than a loss in day care services available to the poor.

Head Start

A major development in public education during recent years has been the recognition that children from poor homes need preschool programs to compensate for their background deficiencies and to bring them closer to the achievement and adjustment levels of their more affluent peers. The Head Start program was initiated under the 1964 Economic Opportunity Act to meet this need and has become the largest public child care and development program. Focusing on four- and five-year-old children, the program served nearly 400,000 children in 1980 at a total cost of $735 million.

Despite the rapid growth of the Head Start program, the vast majority of children from low-income households remain without the benfit of compensatory preschool education. In 1980, Head Start managed to serve only about 20 percent of all eligible children, a proportion that has remained constant since the mid-1970s. Even among the one in five children actually participating in the program, the majority attend for only part of the day. If all eligible children who could participate in Head Start were served in full-year programs, the price tag would exceed $3 billion, an indication of the overwhelming size of the challenge in attempting to reach a larger segment of poor children prior to their entrance into traditional public elementary schools.

While congressional appropriations for the Head Start program have barely kept pace with inflation, the program has continued to offer unique and important educational support to poor children. Because Head Start pupils have serious deficiencies that require individual attention, the program has a lower than usual student-teacher ratio. Like other antipoverty efforts, the program has emphasized the employment of subprofessionals and volunteers to relieve the teacher's work load and provide additional attention to the child. Many of these workers are mothers of children participating in the program. Parental involvement is a major goal of the Head Start effort. A child's needs cannot be met without parental cooperation and it is hoped that beneficial changes in the home environment may be a spin-off effect of the program. Bringing parents into the day-to-day operation of the centers has proved an effective way to advise parents about childrearing practices and to increase their interest in their children's education.

It has been argued that the current educational system acts as a sorting device rather than an equalizing system. Education services are delivered more effectively to children of well-educated and affluent parents than to those of poor parents. Whether Head Start is successful depends ultimately on whether it can induce changes in the American public school system and lessen deleterious influences in home life. More than a shift of goals is necessary, for substantial funds are required for the program's continuation. It has been estimated that the cost of compensatory education runs twice as high as the education of children from affluent homes. Indeed, the financial commitment necessary to realize Head Start's goal of quality education for the poor may conceivably lie beyond realistic expectations for the immediate years ahead.

Nevertheless, the Head Start program has made a significant contribution, dramatizing the educational needs of the poor and offering a program package for dealing with the problems of children from low-income households. The program has helped disadvantaged children "catch up" with their peers and has challenged local school boards that may have lacked the understanding, concern, or commitment to cope with their special needs. While compensatory education efforts such as Head Start are expensive propositions, they remain one of the soundest investments in the future of the next generation.

In an endeavor to provide continuity of effort, Congress authorized a Follow Through program in 1967 to extend Head Start services into the early years of primary school. Because the Follow Through program has never enjoyed the congressional support that has maintained Head Start appropriations in recent years, the exploration of extended education services has been limited to a series of pilot projects testing the effectiveness of differing educational strategies. Yet in the face of uncertain political odds, Congress reauthorized the Follow Through program in 1978 and expanded eligibility to include children who participated in federally assisted preschool programs other than Head Start. Throughout the latter half of the 1970s, annual appropriations have remained static at approximately $60 million.

EDUCATION

While the special education needs of children of the poor have shaped only one aspect of federal child care efforts during the preschool years, the commitment to equal educational opportunity for children from all economic backgrounds has provided the fundamental rationale for federal involvement in what is still perceived as a state and local responsibility. In particular, federal programs have responded to the needs of poor neighborhoods where elementary and secondary schools are typically deficient in resources, facilities, and personnel, and to the special needs, both financial and supportive, of children from low-income households who wish to pursue higher education.

In 1980 the federal government expended $12.5 billion for educational programs. Most of these programs were targeted at serving the poor, handicapped, and minorities, although direct federal assistance to college students is aimed at a much broader clientele and many of the other resources frequently miss their target. Nonetheless, it is estimated that more than one-third of the federal education outlays did reach the poor (table 5).

Elementary and Secondary

The Elementary and Secondary Education Act (ESEA) of 1965 is the primary vehicle for federal aid to the disadvantaged within the nation's public schools. By far the most important initiative under ESEA is the Title I program for compensatory education, which offers aid to state and local programs for educationally disadvantaged students residing in school districts with high concentrations of children from low-income families. While the great majority of Title I funds are distributed to local educational agencies to supplement programs for students in low-income areas, funds are also available for state-operated programs serving handicapped, migrant, neglected, and delinquent children. In 1980, Title I provided $2.8 billion of educational aid to school districts enrolling large numbers of poor children. An additional $435 million was expended in grants to states to help children in state-operated institutions.

Unlike Head Start, which distributes funds on a project-by-project basis with detailed guidelines for localities to follow, Title I funds are distributed in a block grant to state educational authorities, who then allocate them mostly to primary schools, with only an insignificant proportion going to secondary schools. The average expenditure of $466 per child was utilized for additional education materials, teacher's aides, speech and reading specialists, and other services to assist six million children.

Table 5. Estimated federal investment in education for the poor, fiscal 1980

	Total outlays	Estimated outlays for poor
	(millions)	
Total	*$12,529*	*$4,682*
Elementary and secondary		
Early childhood	735	632
Elementary and secondary	3,331	1,699
Emergency school aid	270	57
Other	805	169
Higher education		
TRIO programs	148	120
Student financial assistance	2,709	1,002
Student loan program	1,922	384
Work study	550	182
Other		
Vocational education	784	102
Adult education	105	66
Indian education	76	33
Handicapped	1,049	210
Educational personnel training		
(teacher corps/center)	45	26

Source: Budget of the United States, 1981

Given the immense magnitude of the Title I undertaking—representing nearly one-third of all federal support for education programs serving poor children—the question of the effectiveness of this approach to compensatory education has drawn unwavering and sustained interest since its inception. The program structure itself has generated some legitimate criticisms regarding the use of Title I funds. While federal aid is available only to local educational agencies serving areas with high concentrations of poor children, the funds may be used to assist any student who is "educationally deprived," regardless of family income. Although the intent of avoiding income segregation in schools is laudable, the provisions of the law have created grave obstacles to the effective monitoring of the use of Title I funds at the local level. A recent Office of Education study of Title I showed that the program actually serves more children who are not from poor families than it does low-income or AFDC children, and that a majority of participants cannot even be classified as "low achievers" when compared to their peers. This problem is more disturbing when it is considered that the program serves only an estimated one-third to one-half of all children who need compensatory instruction, and that many of those served do not receive the full range of services they might require. Even though funds have been used to help nonpoor children or have been misdirected for other purposes, ESEA has directed needed funds into districts where the poor concentrate and has opened possibilities for compensatory education.

Postsecondary

Although its value in the marketplace may be diminishing, the sheepskin is still one of the surest avenues out of poverty. Yet, as in many areas, poverty itself is the greatest barrier to participation in higher education. Less than 23 percent of youths from families with incomes below $9,000 attend college, compared to over one-third of youths from families with incomes between $9,000 and $18,000 and over half those with families with incomes above $18,000 (figure 15). These financial college enrollment data are an indication of the obstacle course facing poor youth, in which insufficient money, motivational supports, and prior education combine to discourage the children of the poor from attending college. It was in response to these barriers to a college education that the TRIO programs administered by the Department of Education—Upward Bound, Talent Search, Special Services, and the Educational Opportunity Centers—were created.

The Upward Bound program seeks to motivate students early in their high school careers and to help set their sights on college. Institutions of higher education receive grants to offer summer training and remedial education, including residence on a college compus as well as tutoring throughout the school year. Most students enter after the tenth or eleventh grade and attend two or three summer sessions before entering college.

Similar to all TRIO programs, the target population for Upward Bound is defined by statute to include "first generation college students" whose parents do not have a college degree and "low-income students" whose families have incomes below 150 percent of the poverty level. Yet even with federal outlays of $62.5 million in 1980, Upward Bound has been able to serve only a fraction of the students that might benefit from participation in the program. Under these circumstances, it is not surprising that administrators have chosen the most promising students for enrollment in Upward Bound.

Figure 15 College enrollment and annual family income, 1977

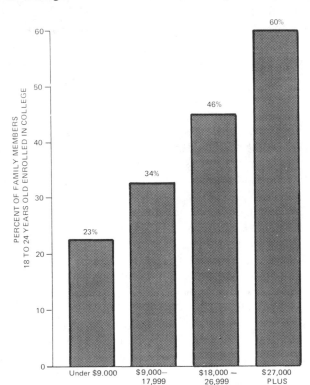

SOURCE: U.S. Bureau of the Census

Notwithstanding these concerns, Upward Bound has produced some encouraging results. Nearly six of every ten Upward Bound high school graduates have entered college. More importantly, at least 60 percent of those who enrolled in college in 1976 were still in attendance two years later, indicating that Upward Bound students are as likely to remain in college as students from more affluent backgrounds. The effectiveness of Upward Bound also suggests that the program has selected students with maximum potential. If funds were available to help more youths from poor homes, the proportion entering college would undoubtedly drop. While the program is rarely able to overcome large educational deficiencies from earlier years, it appears that Upward Bound is an effective mechanism for bolstering student motivation and providing the extra support necessary to guide poor youth into postsecondary education.

Talent Search and the more recent Educational Opportunity Centers—adding a fourth component to the TRIO, although the old nomenclature persists—attempt to develop community-based programs that promote participation in college education. Talent Search focuses on the identification of poor youths with exceptional potential for higher education, while the Educational Opportunity Centers fulfill a similar role in providing adults with information on educational opportunities and supportive and financial assistance services. In 1980 expenditures for both programs totaled $23 million.

A related program, Special Services for Disadvantaged Students, is designed to help poor youths remain in college once they get there. Projects focus on remedial, tutorial, and counseling programs designed to assist students in meeting postsecondary academic standards. In 1980 approximately 210,000 students, about one-third of those eligible, received such services at a cost of $60 million.

In providing a comprehensive range of services that attempts to lower diverse barriers to higher education, the TRIO programs are the most targeted federal effort to assist youth from poor families. Yet in spite of the importance of these support services to educational opportunity, their impact would be minimal in the absence of the much broader and far more expensive commitment to student financial assistance. Federal programs offering grants, loans, and work to low- and middle-income students have grown rapidly in recent years, rising to a total of $5.2 billion in 1980. Reaching over five million students, the rapid expansion of federal student aid has dramatically reduced the financial barriers to opportunities in postsecondary education.

The greatest strides in financial aid have been made since 1972, when amendments to the Higher Education Act created the Basic Educational Opportunity Grant (BEOG) program. Authorizing a maximum award of $1,800 or one-half the cost of attendance (whichever is less), the basic grants have become the cornerstone of federal support for low-income students in postsecondary education.

In 1979, over 1.7 million students received BEOG support, with an average grant award of $866; 42 percent of all benefits went to recipients in families with incomes below $10,000.

In addition to the BEOG program, Congress has established supplemental grant programs intended to assist students attending high-cost institutions and to encourage states to match federal funds for student financial aid. The program, offering a maximum award of $1,500 and administered by institutions of higher education that receive allotments of federal funds based on student population and need, assisted 500,000 students in 1980, with an outlay of $370 million.

The federal college work-study program offers another source of financial support to needy students, allowing participants to earn up to $200 in excess of demonstrated financial need, with the federal government covering up to 80 percent of the cost. Most institutions of higher education participate in the program, with students working up to 15 hours per week during the academic year and up to 40 hours per week in summer work programs. The rates of pay are set by the institutions themselves, although the 1980 amendments to the Higher Education Act prohibit the payment of subminimum wages in programs. A total of $550 million in federal outlays was devoted to college work-study programs serving approximately one million students in 1980.

To supplement direct financial assistance, the National Direct Student Loan program extends long-term loans to low-income students at 3 percent annual interest. The Guaranteed Student Loan program is not intended to serve the poor, but is part of an overall strategy set by Congress with the goal of meeting 75 percent of a student's cost of education through a combination of family contribution and grant aid. In 1980, the federal government spent nearly $2 billion on student loan programs.

Of course, the entire range of student grant and loan programs only represents a portion of federal support for poor youth in higher education. Measured either by outlays or by numbers of students served, the GI bill remains one of the most massive federal commitments to student financial assistance in higher education and must be recognized as a key vehicle for the advancement of poor youth. Federal and state governments also continue to make major investments in institutional aid, and the lower student costs in state-supported colleges and universities in particular can be directly traced to these indirect approaches to subsidized education.

In reviewing the comprehensive system of student financial aid not supported under federal education programs, it is tempting to assume that financial need is no longer a major barrier to participation in higher education in the United States. Even if we have reached this goal at the start of the 1980s, however, it is impossible to ignore the ominous forces that threaten to destroy the ability of the federal government to support this extensive financial aid system as the decade continues. With predictions of sharp declines in college enrollments during the 1980s, the temptation to cut federal aid may gather support. But with cost increases approaching 15 to 20 percent annually, demands for additional federal support of student aid are likely to mount. In addition, the adequacy of federal aid to poor youth is threatened by the gradual extension of student grants and loans to middle-income families—in 1978, a broad effort in Congress to authorize college tuition tax credits was defeated only through passage of a provision that significantly extends eligibility in federal student aid programs. This combination of sharply rising educational costs and a political mandate for a broader distribution of student aid funds have the potential for undermining federal efforts to meet the financial needs of poor youth in the 1980s, and yet there is no doubt that the advances of the past decade have gone a long way toward enabling aspiring youths from impoverished homes to complete a college education.

ADDITIONAL READINGS

Carnegie Council on Policy Studies in Higher Education. *Giving Youth A Better Chance.* San Francisco: Jossey-Bass Publishers, 1979.

Committee for Economic Development. *Education for the Urban Disadvantaged, from Preschool to Employment.* New York: CED, 1971.

Levitan, Sar A., and Alderman, Karen Cleary. *Child Care and ABCs Too.* Baltimore: Johns Hopkins University Press, 1975.

113

Mosteller, Frederick, and Moynihan, Daniel P., eds. *On Equality of Educational Opportunity*. New York: Vintage Books, 1972.
Rossi, Robert J. *Summaries of Major Title I Evaluations*. Palo Alto, Calif.: American Institute for Research, 1977.

DISCUSSION QUESTIONS

1. Evaluate critically the claim that free birth control services are the most cost-effective means to fight poverty.
2. Do you believe that child care is an effective tool to combat poverty?
3. Explain the rationale for compensatory education and the TRIO programs.
4. Granted that a sheepskin is a passport out of poverty, should the federal government undertake the responsibility of subsidizing higher education?
5. Based on the experiences drawn from federal social welfare programs discussed in the preceding three chapters, discuss the strengths and weaknesses of cash transfers and in-kind aid in attacking social programs.
6. "The myriad of social welfare schemes to alleviate proverty is not only costly but is a disincentive to work. The only way to get people off of 'welfare rolls' and onto 'payrolls' is to work through the marketplace by offering businesses tax incentives to hire disadvantaged workers most in need." Comment.
7. What proposals, if any, would you offer for mitigating poverty in the United States and why?

5

Programs for the Working Poor

Anticipate charity by preventing poverty; assist the reduced fellowman . . . so that he may earn an honest livelihood, and not be forced to the dreadful alternative of holding out his hand for charity. This is the highest step and the summit of charity's golden ladder.

—Moses ben Maimon

The goal of the antipoverty programs as stated in the preamble of the Economic Opportunity Act of 1964 "is . . . to eliminate the paradox of poverty in the midst of plenty in this Nation by opening to everyone the opportunity to live in decency and dignity." In order to carry out this goal, more is needed than direct cash payments and the provision of goods and services that might lessen the burden of poverty but fail to attack the causes of dependency. Programs that provide opportunities for self-support and permanent exits from poverty are crucial to its elimination in the long run. As an old proverb moralizes, "Give a man a fish and you feed him for a day. Teach him to catch a fish and you feed him for life."

Those in need of self-help programs are found in a variety of situations. Some of the unemployed lack the skills to compete effectively in the labor market, and others are qualified workers unable to locate a demand for their skill. There are also some, not counted among the unemployed, who are too discouraged by their failure to find work to continue to look. In addition, there are employed persons counted among the "working poor." They are part-time workers who need full-time work to keep them out of poverty and persons employed at such low wages that even full-time work does not raise them above the poverty standard. These underemployed and low earners, when added to the unemployed and discouraged, constitute the "subemployed." The subemployment rate may be more than double the reported unemployment rate, and it gives a more realistic indication of the universe of need for employment and training services.

The range of self-help programs for the employable poor is wide. Some programs focus on the supply side of the labor market, preparing the poor for gainful employment. These include the majority of the employment and training programs launched in the 1960s. Other programs are directed to the demand side, opening doors for the poor in the private labor market and providing public employment for those who are not absorbed in the private sector. A third group of programs seeks to improve the functioning of the labor market for the poor, matching up supply and demand more effectively and setting standards and minimums for low-income employment. Finally, several programs deal with all three of these aspects of the labor market, but concentrate on a specific geographical area or population group.

EMPLOYMENT AND TRAINING

In attempts to help the structurally unemployed and to induce the poor to enter the labor market, the federal government has sponsored a number of employment and training programs responding to their various employment needs. Although not all the programs are specifically targeted at the poor, poverty households are the prime beneficiaries of many of the services offered. These programs provide a wide variety of labor market services and carry a substantial price tag—amounting in 1980 to $14 billion (figure 16). They include efforts directed to specific categories of clients as well as comprehensive programs with broad eligibility criteria. In varying combinations, the following labor market services are offered:

1. outreach to identify the untrained and undermotivated as well as intake and assessment to evaluate their needs and abilities;
2. adult basic education to remedy the absence or obsolescence of earlier schooling;

Figure 16 Federal outlays for employment and training programs by type of service

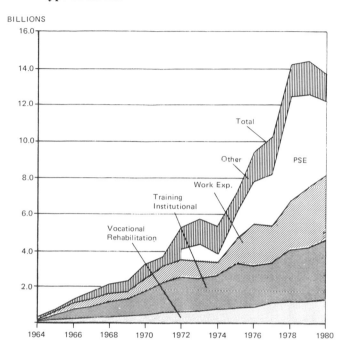

SOURCE: *The U.S. Budget in Brief, Fiscal Year 1981*

3. prevocational orientation to expose those of limited experience to alternative occupational choices;
4. residential facilities for those who live in sparsely populated areas or who live in a debilitating environment that would adversely affect attempts to overcome their disadvantages;
5. work experience for those unaccustomed to the discipline of the work place;
6. creation of public service jobs to upgrade the skills of the disadvantaged until they can compete for permanent public careers;
7. countercyclical creation of public employment opportunities to absorb jobless workers in a high-unemployment economy;
8. job development and subsidized private employment;

117

9. job placement and labor market information services;
10. training allowances to provide support and incentives for those undergoing training; and
11. supportive services—such as medical aid and child care centers for mothers with small children—for those who need assistance to facilitate entry into the labor market or resumption of work.

Few programs, if any, offer all the listed services, but there is a continuing effort to provide comprehensive services to participants and to coordinate complementary programs. Often, however, participants do not receive the precise package they need and may be ineligible or unaware of needed programs because of their diversity. Nevertheless, evidence suggests that those who are served can benefit substantially from the programs.

The majority of the participants in the program received assistance in finding jobs, although frequently the jobs were only temporary. The largest federal outlays were appropriated for job creation. The 1979 distribution of participants in federally funded employment and training services, excluding vocational education, by program follows:

Total (in thousands)	**7,802**
Skill training	827
Institutional	617
On-the-job	210
Job creation	1,480
Work experience	542
Public service	938
Job services	5,008
Job placement	4,537
Career exploration	471
Vocational rehabilitation	487

Often, the poor lack adequate knowledge of the labor market and the contacts needed to secure jobs related to their skills. Job development, information on available opportunities, and referral service to employers increase their likelihood of finding employment. Basic education, vocational training, counseling, and work experience help make the poor more attractive to potential employers. According to the services provided, current employment and training programs can be divided into three major groups: those that emphasize training (including remediation), those that stress work experience and job creation, and those that focus on matching job seekers with appropriate employment opportunities. Some of the programs are designated to specific population segments and provide overlapping services in attempting to meet program goals.

Skill Training

Vocational education is the oldest federal investment in job-related training, dating back to 1917. Federal expenditures in fiscal 1980 totaled about $562 million, and state and local governments contributed over eight times as much. Three-fourths of the federal share was for matching grants to states for basic vocational education programs; the rest supported grants to states for consumer and homemaking education, work-study, cooperative education, vocational research, and other specific activities. Most of the federal money is distributed in grants to state governments, which then parcel it out to local school districts. State and local officials traditionally had wide latitude in spending these funds. In an attempt to gain some control, Congress required in the 1968 Vocational Education Amendments that 15 percent of the state grant be spent for disadvantaged and another 10 percent for handicapped students. However, most school systems have tended to define *disadvantaged* broadly and have included many students who do not come from poor families. Inadequate records are kept by the states about students or program characteristics. Futhermore, some states have not been careful to restrict these funds to the designated students. Thus, help for the poor probably has not yet matched congressional intent.

In addition to these earmarked funds are the regular classes, which enroll the bulk of the students. Because students from poor families are considerably more likely to enroll in vocational curriculum and are less likely to continue their education beyond high school, it is important that vocational courses that would qualify them for jobs be available to them. Although enrollments have been shifting toward more saleable skills, many students attend schools that offer few choices and quite a few are enrolled in courses that may offer little job-related training. It is important that vocational education keep pace with the rapidly changing job market in order to provide useful skills.

Many vocational education enrollees are adults and most are not poor. The educational needs of poor adults are more directly addressed by the $159 million adult education program designated for

119

persons 16 years and older who lack a high school education. Because over one-third of the heads of poor families have completed only eight years of school or less and an additional one-fourth have less than a high school education, it is obvious that the poor form a large proportion of the more than 2 million enrollees in adult education courses. A number of the enrollees go on to job training programs, and many others benefit directly from their educational improvements by higher income.

The initial focus of skill training programs in the 1960s was to retrain workers whose skills had become obsolescent as a result of changing technology. The Manpower Development and Training Act (MDTA) of 1962 provided institutional training for the unemployed and underemployed. However, it became apparent that workers at the margin of the labor force, including a growing number of new entrants, with little or no job skills, were even more in need of training. The institutional programs were expanded to include basic education, training allowances were increased in both amount and duration, and skills centers were established in some 80 communities to provide institutional training in a variety of occupations along with supportive services. Follow-up studies show that most enrollees benefited from their training experience. They experienced less unemployment than control groups, and their earnings increased. The antipoverty efforts of the 1960s spawned a wide variety of programs as new problems were recognized, and by the early 1970s there was a clear need to consolidate and coordinate the diverse efforts. The Comprehensive Employment and Training Act (CETA) of 1973, reauthorized in 1978, was enacted to remove federal restrictions on program structure and to vest greater planning and implementing authority in state and local governments. The resulting federal-state-local partnership has allowed increased flexibility at the local level to develop employment and training services to respond to local labor market needs. The CETA programs provide essentially the same basic services offered under the MDTA programs with each local program deciding the service mix needed and how it is to be provided. Many of the skill centers still operate under contract with local authorities.

A major concern of the 1964 antipoverty law was the employment of youth as the number of teenagers entering the labor market grew rapidly during the 1960s. The Job Corps, established by the

Economic Opportunity Act of 1964, provides intensive and expensive vocational training and basic education to youths from 14 to 21 years of age who are poor, out of school, and out of work. Largely a residential program, it rests on the assumption that the most seriously disadvantaged young people must be removed from their debilitating home environments before they can be rehabilitated. Almost all Job Corps enrollees are from poor families, and most suffer serious educational deficiencies, which would certainly sentence them to a life of poverty. Many have failed in other training programs or in finding and retaining jobs.

All enrollees receive basic education through teaching techniques especially developed for the illiterate and deficiently educated. On the average, they benefit more from this training than they did from their public schools, with educational achievement approaching public school norms. Vocational training of differing complexity is provided, and the corpsmembers receive a wide variety of supportive services, including room, board, health care, recreation, and meager allowances. The total cost of these services is high—$15,000 per corpsmember year, or in excess of $7,000 per enrollee in 1980—but largely unavoidable if residential training is to be provided to unemployed, out-of-school youth.

An expansion of the Job Corps was authorized as part of the 1977 youth initiative, doubling its capacity to 44,000 slots by 1981. As part of the expansion, advanced career training was added to the options available to corpsmembers showing exceptional achievement. In 1979 the program funded about 2,000 poor youths to attend college, primarily in junior and community colleges, or to receive industrial work experience after at least 90 days of center training.

Benefit-cost studies reveal that the investment in the Job Corps program does pay off. In 1979 the Job Corps served approximately 85,000 youths in nearly 100 centers. Among the 37,400 terminees for whom records were available in early 1980 (three-fourths of the total year's terminees), two-thirds were placed in jobs at an average wage of $3.33 an hour and one of every five entered school or the military. This is a significant achievement after an average of six months of training when it is considered that the bulk of participants were from impoverished homes and half had less than a sixth-grade reading level at enrollment.

Since the end of World War II, the Veterans Administration has administered financial support for veterans who wish to continue their education or training. As of 1977, two separate educational benefit programs have existed for veterans. For those entering the military before January 1, 1977, monthly stipends—amounting in 1980 to $311 for single veterans and $370 for a veteran with one dependent— are available under the GI bill. Persons who entered the military after that date are entitled to participate in a contributory educational assistance program. Under this program, the veteran must have contributed $50 to $75 a month, up to a maximum of $2,700 while in service, in order to be eligible. These funds are matched at a rate of $2 for every $1 by the Veterans Administration if they are used to obtain an education, otherwise they are returned to the veteran. The majority of veterans taking advantage of these benefits enroll in college, though enrollment in vocational, professional, business, and high school is also acceptable. Moreover, the educationally disadvantaged and black veterans have failed to participate in the same proportions as whites and high school graduates. To encourage disadvantaged veterans to benefit from the programs, a 1970 amendment to the law provided that time spent on remedial courses or tutoring to correct an educational deficiency could be added to the entitlement, with no reduction in the 36-month limit on benefits. About 13 percent of the veterans who have benefited from the program have less than a high school education. In September 1978, close to 100,000 Vietnam-era veterans were enrolled in high school level courses under the program.

Job Creation

Job creation—known variously as public service employment or work experience— came into its own in the 1970s as an integral part of employment and training policy. Throughout the 1960s the increasing panoply of programs focused largely on the supply side of the labor market by increasing the employability of the unemployed and underemployed. With a few notable exceptions, there was little attention to the demand side, that is, increasing the number of jobs for those available for work.

The largest job creation effort during the 1960s was the Neighborhood Youth Corps, established under the Economic Opportunity Act, which consisted of three separate but related programs aimed at providing work experience and income support for poor youths:

summer and in-school programs to provide jobs and income with the hope of encouraging youths to remain in school, and an out-of-school program that provided an "aging vat" as well as some training for high school dropouts.

Enactment of the Comprehensive Employment and Training Act in 1973 made little immediate change in these job-creation efforts. The federal government continued to provide funds specifically for summer youth programs (nearly a billion dollars in 1979) and an ongoing ($400 million a year) public employment effort for the structurally unemployed.

High unemployment in the mid-1970s led to enactment in 1974 of a much larger public service employment (PSE) program under CETA aimed at the recession's victims. The program was expanded under the Carter administration, peaking at an enrollment of some 750,000 in 1978. By early 1980 overall economic conditions and budgetary constraints forced a retrenchment of the program to about 400,000. In 1979 a total of 543,300 persons benefited from these jobs. Another 370,800 received temporary employment under the CETA job program for the structurally unemployed. To focus on the needs of the poorly educated and unskilled, eligibility had been limited to long-term unemployed from low-income households. More than eight in ten of the 1979 CETA job recipients reported family incomes at or below the poverty level or were otherwise eligible for public assistance.

Although not exclusively a job-creation effort, the youth employment program of 1977, with an initial budget of $1 billion, was passed to reduce youth unemployment, which had remained a major problem during the loose labor markets of the 1970s. In 1979 over 450,000 youths, including more than 100,000 high school dropouts, received work experience, on-the-job training, and other services. The Young Adult Conservation Corps, sponsored by the same act, offers additional employment opportunities for unemployed youth to work in conservation projects on public lands and waterways.

Job Service

Besides the shortage of jobs and lack of skills, the employable poor also suffer because they are unaware both of existing employment opportunities and of training programs. The labor market does not perfectly coordinate jobs with workers, and its inefficiencies are most noticeable in serving poor people.

The largest single delivery system of labor market services is the United States Employment Service (USES). Its 2,500 local offices placed 4.5 million individuals in 1979, including 1.5 million poor persons. Disadvantaged applicants have constituted close to one-fifth of the total in each year since 1968, when the statistics were first collected. One reason for the overrepresentation of the disadvantaged recently has been the "work text" of the food stamp, welfare, and unemployment insurance programs, which require employable applicants to register for work at the USES. Though federally financed, the USES is administered separately in each state. As a result, services to the poor may vary significantly from state to state and from local office to local office.

The Great Society antipoverty efforts shifted the emphasis and responsibilities of the public employment offices toward aid for the poor. The volume of USES activity declined largely because of this shift in emphasis away from serving employers and toward helping the disadvantaged. In the 1970s the ES attempted to rebuild its employer services by reaching out to nondisadvantaged applicants who could fill more of the available job opportunities and by advertising the benefits of this free "job service" to employers to secure more listings. A massive effort was made to improve job matching by computerizing data processing. But as a result of the registration requirements, the unemployed and the poor constitute the bulk of the public employment service clientele.

As the public employment service was attempting through more efficient management to regain its former position in the labor market, the enactment in 1973 of CETA created a new obstacle. The employment service had been the presumptive deliverer of outreach, counseling, placement, and other services prior to 1973. But state and local officials funded under CETA have the option of using other organizations to provide these services. The employment service accordingly lost some grounds, especially in urban areas. Despite the conflicts that grew between the two agencies, accommodations and attempts to coordinate overlapping efforts emerged by the close of the 1970s. But in many localities, possibly the majority, the decentralization and decategorization under CETA effected little substantial change.

Work Incentive Program

The Work Incentive (WIN) program is the culmination of efforts since the early 1960s to induce welfare recipients to achieve economic independence and to stem the growth of welfare. Experience has shown the difficulty of achieving these goals. Enacted as a 1967 amendment to the Social Security Act, WIN began by promising needed comprehensive services to each enrollee. Because enrollees often needed basic education and skill training as well as child care and other supportive services, success was modest and costs were high. Indeed, many "graduates" did not earn enough to leave the welfare rolls.

In reaction to such limited results, the Talmadge amendments, which took effect beginning in 1973, increased federal matching to make the program more attractive to states, and deemphasized classroom training in favor of direct job placement. In the succeeding years the proportion of funds spent on skill training dropped steadily, while the proportion spent on job placement rose, transforming WIN into a delivery agency rather than a training organization. Classroom training, which accounted for nearly all the training expenditures in fiscal 1972, comprised only one-sixth of the 1980 total, and registration for work and direct job placement, including subsidized employment, accounted for over half of the 1980 total outlays.

In fiscal 1978 over 500,000 persons were referred for registration and development of employability plans, and an estimated 200,000 persons were placed in jobs, but many of these persons would probably have found jobs on their own. Because WIN provides little upgrading of enrollees, even those who are placed in jobs leave the program with the same meager skills with which they started. By 1980 total expenditures were $365 million, including $118 million for child care and other services.

The Carter administration welfare reform plan proposed to designate 400,000 CETA job and training slots for AFDC recipients. Again, the program emphasis is on immediate employment and includes an eight-week job search before placing the participant into a subsidized job. As proposed, only a limited proportion of the targeted slots could be used for training, which is essential if the skill level and employment potential of welfare clients are to be improved. The more stringent work requirements backed up by the federal dollar could possibly encourage some households to leave the rolls, but it is improbable that they will lower welfare costs or provide a permanent exit from poverty and dependence.

Vocational Rehabilitation

Job training as well as medical, educational, and other needed services are offered to the physically and mentally handicapped under the federally supported vocational rehabilitation programs. During 1979, close to 500,000 persons received such services, and 300,000 were rehabilitated. In 1965 impoverishment was included as a disabling handicap. It was reasoned that the case-by-case approach of vocational rehabilitation, which provides a variety of services according to individual needs, would prove an effective means of preparing disadvantaged people for satisfactory employment. While few persons are selected on the basis of poverty alone, many of the disabled are poor.

The vocational rehabilitation program has played a significant role in preventing poverty. Over half of the participants in the program were placed in jobs with a significant average increase in income and an additional tenth improved their homemaking capability. One can only speculate whether the successes of the vocational rehabilitation program would be achieved if it were extended to more of the severely disabled with low incomes or to poor persons in general, but the existing program is effectively enhancing the employability of a large number of physically and mentally handicapped poor people, and it is preventing others from becoming economically dependent.

EQUAL OPPORTUNITY IN EMPLOYMENT

Job discrimination has been a major cause of poverty among families headed by females, blacks, Hispanics, and other minority groups. Some among the poor have been denied jobs or advancement solely because of their sex, race, or national origin. Title VII of the Civil Rights Act of 1964 bans discriminatory employment practices by employers, labor organizations, registered apprenticeship programs, and employment services hiring or serving 15 or more persons. In 1972 coverage was expanded to public as well as private employers. The five-member Equal Employment Opportunity Commission (EEOC) was created to implement Title VII. Initially charged with processing complaints on a case-by-case basis and constrained to seek settlements through voluntary compliance, the EEOC's powers were extended by Congress in 1972 to permit lawsuits against respondents charged with violation of the law.

The courts have also broadened the definition of discrimination and clarified what constitutes unlawful employment practices. In 1979 the Supreme Court held that race-conscious affirmative action plans were permitted where designed to overcome *de facto* racial imbalances in an employer's workforce. Until then, all employment preferences based on race were uniformly regarded as illegal.

The Supreme Court had earlier ruled that practices that were fair in form, but resulted in the disparate exclusion of minorities or women, violated the statute. Specifically, it outlawed preemployment tests that were not job-related, permitting only those selection devices or procedures that fairly predicted a job applicant's performance.

Though the EEOC has never been granted power to issue cease-and-desist orders against employers, it has steadily expanded its size and enforcement activities. Potentially most significant was the adoption in 1978 of the enforcement strategy focusing on "systems of discrimination." Under this approach, employment practices resulting in empirically measurable underutilization of minorities or women constitute a violation, leading to legal action by the agency. Class actions on behalf of groups of employees have produced multimillion consent decree agreements with American Telephone and Telegraph Company, General Electric Company, and other major firms.

Another approach is to use the substantial market leverage of the government to bring about compliance with nondiscrimination in employment. The Office of Federal Contract Compliance Programs (OFCCP) requires all firms providing goods or services to the government to establish affirmative action goals and timetables. The major focus originally was in construction, with "hometown plans" in many large cities developed to increase the employment of minority craft workers by contractors. Minority hiring at union wage levels has increased in most crafts, although employment in proportion to minority availability in most local area labor markets has not yet been reached.

In recent years OFCCP has broadened its enforcement activity, after absorbing the contractor-monitoring duties previously fragmented in twelve other federal agencies. By 1979 a wide range of industries and firms were targeted for investigation, particularly contractors in the drug, glass manufacturing, and banking fields. OFCCP's ultimate weapon, the debarment of firms from government contracts, is a strong incentive to promote employment opportunities for minority workers. While this sanction has been used only in isolated cases, its presence is largely behind the increased hiring over the past decade of blacks and other minorities by firms doing business with the federal government.

MINIMUM WAGES

The persistence of poverty among the working poor testifies to the maldistribution of societal rewards for work and the need for improvement. A job—even full-time employment—is not a sure escape from poverty. In 1978 about 6.6 million workers in the labor force did not have high enough earnings to rise above the poverty level. In 1980 a worker would have had to earn at least $3.75 an hour (assuming that the employee worked more than 2,000 hours annually) to lift a family of four out of destitution. However, nearly 5 million adults were employed at or below the minimum wage, which stood at $3.10 an hour in 1980.

Though most of these low-paying jobs are filled on a part-time basis by secondary earners or by youths, there is also a significant number of family heads who work regularly but are unable to escape poverty. In 1978, almost 1 million poor family heads held down a full-time, full-year job. There were also 243,000 unrelated individuals working full time, full year, but remaining in poverty (figure 17). To rise above the poverty line they would need to receive higher hourly wages.

The plight of these adult working poor receives little attention in the training and public employment programs already described. These programs tend to be preoccupied with the unemployed, youth,

Figure 17 Work experience of the poor, 1978

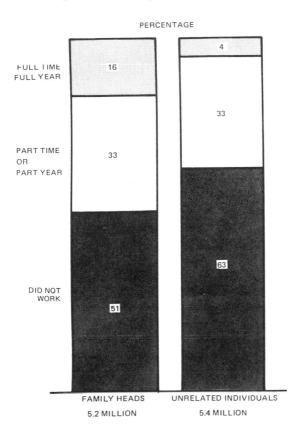

PERCENTAGE

SOURCE: U.S. Bureau of the Census

and those outside the labor force. The goal of most training programs is full-time employment; that this may be no real solution to poverty is often ignored, as are the needs of those who are already laboring at full-time, low-paying jobs.

The minimum wage is perhaps the most direct and comprehensive measure to increase the earnings of the working poor. The objective of the Fair Labor Standards Act of 1938 was to achieve, as rapidly as

129

practicable, minimum wage levels that would sustain the health, efficiency, and general well-being of all workers. An unduly high or rapidly rising minimum might price many low-productivity jobs out of existence, so that the gains from higher wages have to be balanced against the losses from job elimination.

On the assumption that a low-paying job is better than no job at all, Congress has acted incrementally in applying the law over the years. It has established minimum wages that directly affect only a limited number of employees at the bottom of the economic ladder. The 1974 amendments expanded minimum wage protection to an additional 7.4 million workers. The two major groups covered by the 1974 amendments were federal, state, and local employees and most private household workers. But a 1976 Supreme Court decision removed many state and local workers from federal FLSA protection. Additional amendments in 1977 did little to expand coverage further. By 1978 about 60 million workers—close to 85 percent of all nonsupervisory workers—were covered by the minimum wage. Still not covered are 11 million nonsupervisory employees, primarily in retail and wholesale trade, service industries, agriculture, and finance. Though state minimum wage laws provide some protection to excluded workers, these standards range widely and are usually far below the federal minimum wage.

One can only speculate about the number of workers whose earnings are boosted by the minimum wage, but some insights can be gained from reviewing the incremental increases in the minimum wage and extensions in coverage. It was estimated that the 1977 law initially boosted the wages of 4.5 million workers.

The favorable impact of minimum wage rates is reduced to the extent that employers find it unprofitable to retain or hire workers at the government-imposed wage levels, resulting in job loss or reduced work rather than higher earnings. Because many factors are involved, it is difficult to determine the extent of job elimination. The available evidence indicates that the minimum wage legislation has raised the total income of the poor, and that any losses in employment and earnings were more than compensated by the increased earnings of the majority. This is, of course, little comfort to individuals who lost their jobs as a result of such increases. Nor do studies of changes affecting those presently employed tell the whole story. Future demand for labor might be dampened, closing off potential job opportunities for those who might otherwise have been hired. Some economists claim that the youth unemployment problem is largely the result of minimum wages. If minimum wages were reduced or removed altogether, they argue, more jobs would be created at lower wages. The assertion remains unproven. Statistical research indicates that even if there was no minimum wage, youth unemployment would still have been a serious problem during the 1970s. However, true to the adage that there is no free lunch, the minimum wage does entail some costs. Accordingly, support has developed for a "dual minimum," which would permit a lower minimum, for example, for all youths under 18, or 18- to 19-year-olds in the first six months of employment. During the 1977 congressional round of amendments, the idea of a "dual minimum" lost in the House by only one vote.

It is questionable, however, whether a dual minimum wage would have a significant impact on youth unemployment. A major cause of unemployment among black teenagers and other disadvantaged groups must be sought elsewhere. First, the liberalization and expansion of various income support measures, including Aid to Families with Dependent Children, have offered a minimal measure of income maintenance to young women with children. Some may have preferred to subsist on relief rather than to work at very low wages. Second, many of the potential jobs open to blacks in slum areas disappeared with the exodus of white families. As jobs moved to suburbia, many residents of slum areas became economically stranded, owing to inadequate public transportation or the lack of private "wheels." In other words, some black unemployment reflects suburban housing discrimination. Third, demographic factors and an increased supply of black youths in slum areas must also have contributed to increased unemployment, particularly since, as already suggested, the demand for their labor has declined. Nonetheless, if a significant boost in minimum wages can be purchased at some inflationary cost, the trade-off may be a small price to help reduce the number of working poor. In the final analysis, conclusions regarding the impact of minimum wage legislation upon aggregate employment and unemployment depend on value judgments, and whatever the conclusion some relevant facts can be found to support the views.

To minimize the dangers of unemployment and inflationary pressures, many proponents concede that minimum wages should be raised no more rapidly than average wages in American industry.

While little is known about productivity trends in low-wage industries affected by minimum wage legislation, it is reasonable to assume that the rise in productivity in these industries is no greater than in the rest of the American economy. If this assertion is correct, a rule of thumb might be that boosts in the minimum wage should be no larger than rises in the cost of living, plus average productivity increases.

In an inflationary economy it may be desirable to raise the minimum rate frequently, at least more often than Congress is likely to enact new legislation. One way to adjust the minimum wage to increasing living costs, and to avoid the discontinuities of infrequent but large jumps, is to "index" the minimum to a cost-of-living measure, much as social security and other benefits are now automatically increased. In 1977 Congress rejected a proposal to index minimum wages, but voted instead to raise the hourly minimum to $2.65 in 1978, $2.90 in 1979, $3.10 in 1980, and $3.35 in 1981.

Some experts have argued for setting minimum wage rates high enough to eliminate poverty among all full-time workers. Regrettably such pronouncements are more rhetoric than serious policy alternatives. Reasonable people may differ on whether the current minimum wage should be extended to additional millions of workers or whether it should be kept for a while at the present level or raised by a few cents, but there can be little doubt that excessively rapid boosts in the minimum wage would cause serious economic dislocations and loss of jobs. It would be a case of killing the goose that lays the egg, even if it contains little gold. Eliminating jobs is not the way to fight poverty. Rapid increases in minimum wages, in any event, should be accompanied by a work relief program that would provide employment to displaced workers at the statutory minimum wage rate.

Without diminishing the past achievements of the minimum wage, it would be unrealistic to place excessive reliance upon such legislation as a tool to combat poverty. If society is determined to reduce poverty at a more rapid rate than in the past, additional tools will have to be relied upon.

MIGRANT WORKERS AND ILLEGAL IMMIGRANTS

As a group, migrant workers are one of the most exploited segments of the work force. Most are blacks and Mexican-Americans based in southern Texas, California, and Florida. The average migrant worker has only a fourth or fifth grade education. Living conditions are normally characterized by substandard housing, both in base residence and while traveling. Dilapidated housing, low incomes, and lack of protection from employment-related injury and illness foster poor health conditions. These workers follow the harvest as far north as Minnesota, Washington, and New York each year, often paying farm labor contractors to find them jobs at wages bringing an average annual income considerably below the poverty level.

Because they are on the move from spring until fall each year, migrant workers are difficult to reach through the standard federal social and welfare programs. Residency requirements and difficulties in certifying their incomes limit their access to such programs as Medicaid, food stamps, welfare, and job training. Given their meager incomes, child labor becomes a necessity in defiance of laws designed to keep the children in school.

Employment prospects for migrant workers are declining steadily as more mechanical devices are introduced in the harvesting process. There has been no significant increase in rural nonfarm employment to absorb displaced workers. Moreover, these working poor are not entitled to the protection of federal labor laws providing for unemployment compensation and collective bargaining or of many states' workers' compensation laws. Therefore, the need to train migrant workers and to provide basic education to their children is pressing if the poverty of these families is not to be visited on future generations.

Even the serious problems of migrant laborers are probably not as severe as those of illegal immigrants. Foreign nationals who enter or work in the United States in violation of U.S. immigration laws typically suffer the worst working conditions and the lowest wages of any segment of the labor force. Yet, because these "undocumented workers" (as they have been termed by the United Nations agencies) are deportable aliens, they have few remedies to enable them to protect their constitutional rights, and little access to public aid or support.

While many of these illegal immigrants today come as tourists from the Caribbean, Asia, Africa, and Europe to find unauthorized employment in major metropolitan areas throughout the United

States, the majority illegally cross the 2000-mile United States-Mexico border, often with the help of smugglers. Like virtually all other illegal immigrants, Mexican undocumented workers are at once pulled into the United States by the lure of higher wages and pushed by very low standards of living and the lack of employment opportunities in their native land.

U.S. policy since the turn of this century has alternately discouraged, encouraged, or ignored the flow of illegal Mexican labor into the American Southwest, depending on the health of the U.S. economy and its need for cheap labor. In recent years, however, the number as well as the kind of illegal immigrants entering the United States appear to have increased greatly. Although the enforcement resources of the Immigration and Naturalization Service have not substantially changed, INS apprehensions of illegal immigrants have increased tenfold during the last decade, and an estimated 3 to 6 million are believed to reside in the nation today.

Like our immigrants of times past, the illegal immigrant of today tends to be a young and unskilled adult male, in search of economic opportunity on a scale that he cannot find in his home country. Though the data on this clandestine population are scanty, most illegal immigrants do indeed appear to be "undocumented workers." And despite the fact that nine of ten have less than six years of schooling and speak no English, the work that they obtain is not solely menial minimum-wage jobs. Surveys of apprehended illegals have estimated the proportion employed in farm work at only about one-third, with substantial numbers finding work in manufacturing, construction, and services. This wide range of jobs means that some workers obtain relatively good wages. Although the average hourly wage reported in a 1975 survey of apprehended illegals was only $2.34 when the minimum wage was $2.10, half the illegals caught in Chicago in early 1975 reportedly earned $3.50 or more. While this wage was still below the average for American industry, it does suggest that some illegals hold jobs paying average wage rates or better.

Large numbers of illegal aliens in the labor force and the evidence that they are penetrating a broad range of industries and occupations present a policy dilemma during periods of high national unemployment. Clearly, if there are as many as three to six million illegals working in the country, many of them are holding jobs that could otherwise be filled by some of the nation's unemployed. Because illegals are often willing to work hard under adverse conditions for low wages, they tend to depress wage rates, slow improvements in working conditions, and hamper unionization efforts in agricultural and manufacturing industries, particularly in the southwestern states where they have clustered until the 1970s. Moreover, while illegals themselves may have little access to unemployment insurance, welfare, or other social benefits, their impact on unemployment and wage rates doubtless forces some individuals, who would otherwise have a job to support themselves, to depend on the government for support.

Because of these adverse impacts on the welfare of American workers there have been attempts to strengthen immigration laws. In addition to stepped-up efforts by the Immigration and Naturalization Service, bills introduced in Congress have proposed that employers who hire illegals be penalized (currently there are no sanctions on hiring illegal aliens). At the same time, however, agricultural and industrial interests have claimed that there is a shortage of workers willing to take low-level, low-wage jobs. Efforts to diminish the adverse impact of illegal immigration on the wages and employment opportunities of U.S. workers by enacting employer sanctions have been countered by employer proposals to ensure the availability of low-wage labor by enacting a temporary foreign worker program. Whatever measures are adopted, the difficulties of controlling illegal immigration will remain as long as American borders are relatively open and there are economic incentives for poor Mexicans and those of other nationalities to seek higher-wage U.S. jobs.

Area Development Programs

For a myriad of reasons rooted in regional economic trends and often in unique local conditions, poverty tends to become concentrated in specific geographic locations. Declining employment opportunities, high rates of out-migration, low per capita income, underdeveloped infrastructure, low educational attainment of the population, and a high percentage of farm employment interact in some localities to produce labor surplus or "depressed areas." The areas themselves vary. Poverty pockets exist in otherwise prosperous metropolitan areas, in underdeveloped rural areas, and in isolated or stagnating regions cut off from the rest of the economy. Some are as small as an inner-city neighborhood and some as expansive as Indian reservations or major sections of the rural South. The problems faced by rural and urban areas differ, but are related. The out-migration plaguing many rural areas has resulted in an influx of unskilled migrants into the cities, whose middle and upper classes in turn have fled to the suburbs, creating poverty ghettoes in the inner-cities. Depressed urban and rural areas fail to attract new economic enterprise because they frequently lack adequate public facilities and the labor force tends to be deficiently educated and poorly trained.

While the history of federal efforts to promote area redevelopment can be traced to the New Deal programs of the 1930s, the major federal economic development programs emerged in the 1960s and have received increased emphasis under the Carter administration in the late 1970s. The central thrusts of the economic development effort are directed by the Economic Development Administration and the Department of Housing and Urban Development, although significant efforts also continue under the Department of Interior, the Department of Agriculture, and the Appalachian Regional Commission. Federal outlays in 1980 to aid labor surplus areas were distributed as follows:

	Millions
Total	$6,686
Economic Development Administration (Commerce)	1,074
Community development block grants (HUD)	3,500[1]
Urban development action grants (HUD)	180
Regional commissions	430
Bureau of Indian Affairs (Interior)	846
Rural development and business assistance (Agriculture)	656

[1]While economic development is an acceptable and increasingly dominant activity under the community development block grant program, only an undetermined portion of this total is actually used for that purpose.

The Public Works and Economic Development Act of 1965, administered by the Economic Development Administration of the Department of Commerce, has been the traditional source of economic development funds for local areas with consistently high rates of unemployment. EDA provides grants for public works and other redevelopment projects, industrial development loans, loan guarantees and interest subsidies, technical assistance, and research and development grants. EDA is also authorized to provide aid to workers and firms suffering a negative impact from increased foreign imports under the trade adjustment assistance program. Funding levels for currently authorized activities increased markedly in the late 1970s. The National Public Works and Economic Development Act, which reauthorized EDA in 1980, further expanded the agency's authority to assist local government and private sector programs.

The Department of Housing and Urban Development has also evolved into a major source of federal aid to depressed areas. Community development under HUD is in the form of block grants to state and local governments for supporting initiatives aimed at stabilizing and improving housing for the poor in particular and the community in general. The block grant approach authorized by the Housing and Community Development Act of 1974 allows state and local jurisdictions to exercise their discretion in supporting a variety of urban renewal and community improvement and development activities. With the growing emphasis on federal block grants and local decisionmaking, communities are expected to integrate community development projects with employment projects under the Comprehensive Employment and Training Act.

Congress considered problems of severely distressed urban areas in the Housing and Community Development Act of 1974 and later amendments that authorized urban development action grants (UDAG). A major focus of the UDAG program is to use public funds to encourage private investment in redevelopment projects in poverty areas. In 1980, $180 million was allocated through block grants to designated cities, towns, and urban counties to assist in revitalizing their economic base and reclaiming blighted neighborhoods for renovation.

While both EDA and HUD programs focus primarily on urban areas, the Department of Agriculture provides extensive aid to economically depressed rural areas throughout the country. Authorized by the Rural Development Act of 1972, the Farmers Home Administration administers a major business and industrial loan program channeling, in 1980, $1.0 billion in direct loans and loan guarantees to businesses and local governments in communities with populations below 50,000. FHA also provided $321 million in grants to rural areas for commercial and economic development. Finally, the Rural Electrification Administration has served as the source of capital investment assistance to rural areas since 1936, financing subsidized loans for improved electrical generation and consumer services, and for the improvement and expansion of rural telephone service.

The Appalachian Regional Commission represents a rather unique federal approach to economic development. Created under the Appalachian Regional Development Act of 1965, the commission is authorized to provide a broad range of federal assistance within a 13-state area extending from New York to Mississippi. The use of a regional planning commission to channel economic development funds was unparalleled in federal program administration at its inception. While the 1965 Public Works and Economic Development Act authorized other regional development planning commissions, they have only recently received limited federal funding.

Reflecting the underlying assumption of the legislation that the economic distress of the Appalachian region is due in large part to its relative isolation (and possibly because the several states involved could initially agree on relatively few concrete projects), the majority of the $2.5 billion Congress appropriated for the Appalachian Regional Commission was allocated for the construction of a proposed 2,700-mile highway system and 1,500 miles of access roads. The remainder of the funds is used to increase the federal share in grant programs, to finance health and child-development projects, to create vocational education facilities, to restore the land ravaged by mining, and for other public facilities.

Quite obviously, jobs are created by these direct expenditures; but the long-term effect of improved transportation and infrastructure in attracting industry to the region is not clear. While federal aid to underdeveloped areas may offer significant boosts to local economies, it remains virtually impossible to separate the impact of federal policies from the constant fluctuations of business cycles and regional growth trends. In itself, federal economic development assistance is rarely provided in the massive or concentrated doses necessary to reverse the economic decline of truly distressed areas.

If the role of federal aid in economic development is uncertain, the effectiveness of programs for distressed areas in fighting poverty is even less clear. The federal policies toward distressed areas rely on a "trickle down" approach, concentrating on aid to the business community and assuming that such efforts will translate into new jobs to help the unemployed in the future. While this attempt to provide incentives for businesses to locate or to expand enterprises in high unemployment and poverty areas may be justifiable on other grounds, it is necessarily a long-range strategy with little immediate antipoverty impact. Economic development programs will seldom offer direct relief to the poor, but they may help to minimize disparities in regional growth that can generate high concentrations of low-income households that compound difficulties in alleviating poverty.

Indian Programs

Federal programs for American Indians are a special application of the area approach to poverty. These programs provide a wide range of goods and services as well as income and employment for Indians on reservations. This unusual concentration of federal support is a response to the serious deprivation that exists among the 652,700 Indians who live on 270 federal reservations, and other trustlands, as well as a belated recognition of the government's culpability for the adverse conditions under which Indians live.

The highest incidence of concentrated poverty in the United States is found on Indian reservations. Comparative indicators emphasize this impoverishment. In 1970 Indian families had average incomes two-fifths as large as the average American family. This lower income must be shared by families that include twice as many children under 18 as the national average. Unemployment rates on reservations are several times higher than the national average, and a majority of reservation families live in unsanitary, dilapidated housing. Moreover, the violent crime rate on reservations is nine times that for rural America; Indian schoolchildren drop out before completing high school at a rate double the national average; and the average life span of an Indian is significantly shorter than the national norm. Obviously, reservation Indians desperately need a federal program that employs an area approach to their concentration of poverty.

Because of Indians' unique historical status as wards of the state, the federal government has assumed broader responsibilities for reservation residents than for other citizens. Altogether, the federal government expended close to $1.9 billion on programs for Native Americans, mostly benefiting those living on or near reservations. Besides the estimated $433 million spent by various federal agencies for social welfare and capital improvement projects on reservations, the Indian Health Service and the Bureau of Indian Affairs spent $1,496 million on their programs, not including funds appropriated to settle the claims of Alaskan natives or those from tribal trust funds (figure 18). This amounts to nearly $2,955 for each Indian residing on or near a reservation. While this aid may appear to be large, on the surface it must be noted that the sources of additional funds for Indians are very limited. Lacking significant private resources or economic activity, Indians on reservations must depend upon federal support for essential services and goods.

Figure 18 Federal assistance to Indians, 1979

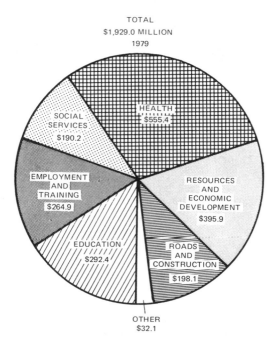

TOTAL
$1,929.0 MILLION
1979

HEALTH
$555.4

SOCIAL
SERVICES
$190.2

EMPLOYMENT
AND
TRAINING
$264.9

RESOURCES
AND
ECONOMIC
DEVELOPMENT
$395.9

EDUCATION
$292.4

ROADS
AND
CONSTRUCTION
$198.1

OTHER
$32.1

SOURCE: *The Budget of the United States Government, Fiscal Year 1981*

Despite the relatively high per capita federal expenditures, the "big brother" approach to solving reservation problems has not worked. The reasons are complex. They include a failure to consider the Indians' cultural heritage, as well as disputes within federal agencies and among the Indians themselves regarding appropriate program goals. Paradoxically, if Indians are ever to free themselves from the federal government, even more federal aid will be necessary to develop their economic base and social institutions. Without this infrastructure, the Indian communities will be unable to contribute support to their own institutions.

ADDITIONAL READINGS

Levitan, Sar A., and Belous, Richard S. *More Than Subsistence: Minimum Wages for the Working Poor.* Baltimore: Johns Hopkins University Press, 1979.

Levitan, Sar A., and Johnston, William B. *Indian Giving.* Baltimore: Johns Hopkins University Press, 1975.

Levitan, Sar A.; Mangum, Garth L.; and Marshall, Ray. *Human Resources and Labor Markets.* New York: Harper and Row, 1980.

Levitan, Sar A., and Taggart, Robert. *Jobs for the Disabled.* Baltimore: Johns Hopkins University Press, 1977.

Levitan, Sar A., and Zickler, Joyce. *Too Little But Not Too Late: Federal Aid to Lagging Areas.* Lexington, Mass.: D.C. Heath and Lexington Books, 1976.

Mangum, Garth L. *Employment and Employability.* Salt Lake City, Utah: Olympus Publishing Company, 1976.

U.S., Commission on Civil Rights. *Social Indicators of Equality for Minorities and Women.* Washington, D.C.: Government Printing Office, 1978.

U.S., Department of Labor. *Employment and Training Report of the President.* Washington, D.C.: Government Printing Office, current year.

DISCUSSION QUESTIONS

1. Summarize the salient facts concerning the impact of welfare upon incentives to work and sketch your favorite scheme for reducing conflicts between work and welfare.

2. A significant phenomenon of recent years has been the increasing overlap between the wage structure and the benefits available from public assistance programs. What are the reasons for this development? What do you see as the consequences? Appraise the political prospects and potential effectiveness of proposals designed to deal with this phenomenon.

3. In what ways can education and training be considered as investment?

4. What role does civil rights legislation play in combating poverty?

5. Reconcile the claims that minimum wage laws eliminate jobs and that they protect the poor by raising their standard of living.

6. What were the economic and social forces, both long and short run, that led to the emergence of employment and training policies and programs during the 1960s and 1970s? In what ways would you expect these programs to change in the next three years?

7. "Rehabilitation, not relief," has been an implicit and explicit credo in U.S. antipoverty efforts. It is largely this emphasis that has so intertwined employment and antipoverty efforts. To what extent are employment and training policies and programs useful as antipoverty tools?

8. Do you believe that the government should consider company hiring and promotion practices in awarding contracts?

9. Discuss the concept of area depression and the problems associated with measuring this phenomenon. In what way are they the same? In what way are they different? What implications do these similarities and differences have for public policy? What public policies are presumably on the books to assist these less developed areas? Are they successful?

10. Analyze the conflict between the goals of Indian self-determination and their status under various treaties with the federal government.

6

Goals and Priorities to Combat Poverty

The needy shall not always be forgotten; the hope of the poor shall not perish for ever.

—Psalms 9:18

THE LESSONS OF THE GREAT SOCIETY

Major strides were taken during the 1960s and 1970s to combat poverty. The Great Society's antipoverty legislation of the 1960s represented our nation's most massive effort to meet the needs of the poor. The strategy was threefold. First, placing emphasis upon the presumed desirability of changing the poor, the Great Society improved the provision of diverse services, focusing on educational opportunities and training. Second, the Great Society legislation aimed to change American institutions to allow the poor a greater voice in determining their own destiny, including the planning and implementation of programs in aid of the poor. Third, the Great Society expanded direct assistance to the poor through the provision of in-kind services, including health care, shelter, and nutrition.

While the rhetoric of the Great Society antipoverty warriors was muted in the 1970s, expansion of aid to the poor continued and most of the antipoverty efforts continued, even though their titles were changed and they were administered under diverse auspices. Of course, this frontal assault on poverty proved to be a uniquely expensive undertaking. Federal expenditures rose sharply under the

Johnson administration, and the entitlements and programs of the Great Society legislation fueled a continuation of rapid budget growth during the first Nixon administration. By 1973, total federal outlays had more than doubled (after adjusting for inflation) in the span of a single decade, accompanied by a growing concern that the "budget explosion" was a prime cause of the inflation that had become the major national problem of the 1970s. The Nixon-Ford administrations moved in the mid-1970s to restrain the growth of the federal budget. Few doubted the need for an end to the rapid expansion of federal outlays; the fight centered primarily on whose ox was to be gored.

Since the programs in aid of the poor had expanded so greatly during the decade, the decision was made that much of the pruning of the budget should also be made in subsidized housing, education, employment and training programs, and related antipoverty efforts. The goal of the Great Society to eliminate poverty was abandoned as rhetoric during the second Nixon administration and succeeding Ford and Carter administrations, although antipoverty expenditures continued to expand. Instead, the prophecy that "the poor ye shall always have with you" received new currency. Continued poverty was seen as an acceptable trade-off to check the expansion of the federal budget with accompanying rising deficits and inflationary pressures.

Underlying the formal deemphasis of antipoverty programs was the recognition that the Great Society's hope for an easy victory over poverty remained elusive and that the most flagrant deprivation had been sharply alleviated. The nation was apparently not willing to sustain the struggle against poverty as a top priority item on the American agenda. Even in this most affluent of societies the antipoverty measures must compete with other national goals. Moreover, experience from the New Deal through the 1970s made it abundantly clear that the eradication of poverty is a costly and complex effort. National policy makers, assigning a lower priority to the poor, decided not to commit the resources necessary to eliminate poverty.

By the beginning of the 1980s, the process had come full circle. The total of federal, state, and local expenditures for social programs reached a peak in 1976 after a generation of growth, representing 20.4 percent of the GNP. This percentage slipped to 19.7 percent in 1977 and then to 19.4 percent in 1978, a clear indication that the welfare system had matured and the level of beneficiaries had stabilized, though expenditures specifically targeted at the poor continued to expand. Also, the automatic cost-of-living adjustments in many current programs prevented a major decline in the relative levels of outlays. The focus of national policy shifted to attempts to reduce inflationary pressures. In this context, an eventual halt to increasing outlays for antipoverty programs was predictable in the absence of new political initiatives in aid of the poor.

It also became clear that the Great Society fell short of creating an orderly program for providing income for the poor. While millions of Americans living in poverty were given additional income through the expansion of public assistance, training stipends, and in-kind measures, a universal system to meet the basic income needs of the poor and to blend that income support with essential services was never developed. Perhaps even more important than massive new federal expenditures, the challenge for the 1980s lies in the development of an integrated approach to reducing poverty, one that treats all segments of the poor equitably while targeting federal resources at those areas or groups with the greatest need and potential.

A Comprehensive Program

A comprehensive program in aid of the poor should recognize that the poor need both income and services, not one or the other. As a reaction against the expansion of services, some antipoverty warriors have come up with a simple solution: "Give them money." This approach was also supported by some conservatives who found the provision of money in line with their ideological preference of minimizing government intervention in the marketplace. While this advice will not go down in history with "Let them eat cake," it may be equally unrealistic. Even more generous, the provision of money alone without institutional changes and needed services will not eradicate poverty. And, given the current climate of opinion, it is not realistic to expect that society will provide enough to eliminate poverty in the foreseeable future.

A useful general rule for allocating additional resources would be to emphasize those efforts that attack the causes of poverty rather than those that merely mitigate its symptoms. Granted that the two objectives are not easily separated, the rule suggests the need for continuing research into the factors that contribute to the persistence of poverty and a commitment to use available resources to strike at the roots of poverty.

The vast experimentation of the past two decades suggests some courses of action for the next decade and beyond. While significant gaps remain in our understanding of the causes of poverty, we need not await returns from all the precincts to continue a vigorous campaign to reduce poverty. Lacking comprehensive knowledge, we can focus on specific measures to aid selected groups among the poor. This suggested emphasis should not necessarily supplant the generalized social goal of eliminating all poverty; a free and affluent society should aim at nothing less. We should realize that this is an ultimate goal, and one of numerous and pressing demands upon society's attentions and resources. Realistically, given the significant advances during the 1960s and 1970s and the pressing problems facing the nation in the early 1980s, for the time being we must forego grand designs for the good society and concentrate on more modest and specialized strategems.

Even assuming that consensus can be reached on the amount of additional resources to be allocated for the attack on poverty, it is not at all clear how these resources should be distributed and most effectively utilized. What share of any additional dollars should be allocated to raising the cash income of the poor as compared with improving the quality and quantity of services that are offered to them? The poor are not a homogeneous mass. Additional income will provide for the basic needs of some; many others require services that will enable them to partake in the affluence of American society. Until these special services and income in kind are adequate, it will be premature to hope for a guaranteed minimum income that would eliminate poverty. Indeed, in view of the multiple problems faced by the poor, it is problematic whether a reasonable cash grant can provide for their basic needs.

Guaranteed Income

In considering steps to provide a base level of guaranteed income for the poor, it would be a mistake to overlook the advances made in the transfer system already in place. While the several existing programs may seem disjointed and inefficient, in sum they form a fairly comprehensive, albeit not universal or uniform, system. Each of the various programs has its own target group, but there are no longer major gaps in coverage, although some duplication is inevitable under the system. The growth of the food stamp program and increased coverage under unemployment compensation have finally extended some aid to the working poor, while the federalization of adult public assistance categories has improved the lot of the disabled and aged who cannot work. These recent improvements in the current transfer system are significant, even if they do not obviate the need for more direct commitment to a guaranteed income.

While the benefits of some minimal income guarantee for those in need have long been recognized, the transition to this more direct transfer system has proved difficult. The classic dilemma for public policy lies in the balance between the minimum income guarantee, work incentives, and total program costs. A grant adequate to supply base needs and an effective tax rate on benefits low enough to preserve work incentives combine to create a very expensive antipoverty program. It was in this context that even the guaranteed income proposals advanced by the Nixon and Carter administrations failed to gain support in Congress—some critics believing that the proposals offered too little support to the destitute; others fearing that a more generous level of guaranteed income would push program costs to unacceptable heights. The problems posed by the need to overhaul the current system of in-kind benefits and to accommodate state and local variations in benefit levels and in living costs also have stymied previous efforts to put a guaranteed income program in effect. Finally, the difficulties of spelling out operational distinctions between employable and unemployable individuals in the treatment of the poor remains a serious obstacle to preserving essential work incentives while also meeting the basic needs of those unable to work.

Notwithstanding these obstacles to the development of a more efficient and equitable income transfer program, recent changes have moved us in the right direction. The plight of the working poor looms as one of the greatest barriers to the elimination of poverty, for any attempt in the present transfer system to raise the nonworking poor out of poverty would only create unacceptable work disincentives for the millions of Americans working and yet still living in poverty or just above the poverty threshold. The Earned Income Tax Credit passed in 1976 and subsequently expanded offers significant relief to the working poor through the tax structure, serving as a wage supplement that builds upon the modest security of minimum wage laws. In addition, the Carter administration has moved to establish a minimum benefit level of 65 percent of the poverty level in the AFDC program, a far cry from a guaranteed income for all Americans but a significant advance in building a base of federal support for the poor.

The crucial step in moving toward a guaranteed income system now is the willingness to accept the added cost of a fair and comprehensive program. A reasonable goal would be a guaranteed income of 70 percent of the poverty threshold ($5,200 per year for a family of four in 1980). In keeping with the guideline that priority should be given to attacking the roots of poverty, cash grants should take the form of income supplements for the working poor, work incentives for other employable poor, and allowances for other households living in poverty. Again, the attempt to ensure that work remains profitable will be difficult and costly, and this goal requires a graduated tax that would withdraw only a portion of benefits as earned income increased. The exact annual added cost of such a plan (1980 prices), though difficult to estimate, would probably exceed $20 billion. In light of the size of this commitment, the transition will necessarily be a gradual one, perhaps beginning with a graduated tax on earnings on top of an initial guaranteed income equal to 60 percent of the poverty level and raising the ante by 2 percent annually for five years. The task is formidable, and yet the cost of even a modest program is a measure of the hardship faced by the portion of the American population still unable to lift themselves out of poverty in the 1980s.

The Nonincome Needs of the Poor

No one has ever managed to design a "neat" system for meeting the multiple needs of the poor, or any other large group. Even if we are able to develop a guaranteed income that reduces some the complexity of the current transfer system, there will remain a broad range of in-kind assistance that cannot be replaced by a cash grant. In developing a strategy for meeting the needs of the poor, federal assistance must be concentrated on those services that have the greatest potential for reaching the causes rather than the symptoms of poverty, serving this generation and the next. While the specific priorities are subject to debate, child care, compensatory education, job training and job creation, family planning, and the strengthening of protective legislation emerge as major areas for federal efforts in the 1980s.

1. Over a century ago the people of the United States reached a consensus that free schooling should be made available to all. While publicly supported education continually expanded, little attention was given to lowering the entry age for poor children in publicly supported schools before the establishment of Head Start. The growing number of working women, including mothers with small children, raises the need to expand preschool facilities on a universal basis. In light of the massive outlays required to establish needed facilities, more affluent parents initially might be required to pay tuition to support such programs while children from poor families are admitted free. In any case, the expansion of child care and education services to preschool children, particularly those with working mothers, should be our first priority as an investment in the next generation during the most formative and important years.

The other priority area for consideration in education must target aid at the improvement of educational quality in elementary and secondary schools, particularly in poverty areas. Remedial education is expensive and, to the extent that the additional investment would make the broader educational system more effective the first time around, federal aid targeted at poor communities can reduce the need for rehabilitative measures. The traditional mode of local school financing places areas of high poverty concentration at a severe disadvantage, and carefully monitored support for the improvement of local educational practice can restore some equity to educational opportunity in basic education. Remedial efforts will no doubt remain important to the poor, and the expansion of opportunities in higher education offers a major escape route from poverty, but efforts in both these areas will prove futile without a sound base of preschool care and elementary and secondary education on which to build.

2. Experience has shown that our economy may not generate an adequate number of jobs to employ selected sectors of the population gainfully. The poorly educated and unskilled are of particular concern to public policy, and creation of jobs for them should be second only to

the establishment of adequate training facilities for those who are sufficiently motivated to acquire new skills. The continued high level of unemployment among the unskilled, particularly among blacks and other minorities, indicates the need to generate government-supported employment—not make-work jobs—for those who cannot qualify for gainful employment in private industry.

Despite the gloomy forebodings by the prophets of cybernation, much of society's needed work is not being done, and the needs are going to increase rather than disappear. Many of these jobs can be performed by relatively unskilled, unemployed workers, whether in rural areas or urban centers. Stream clearance, reforestation, and park maintenance are some of the traditional work-relief jobs. Many new jobs can be added, such as school aides, health aides, simple maintenance jobs in public buildings, and renovation of slum areas. These jobs should be in addition to countercyclical job-creation programs designed to help the victims of economic recession. Creating these jobs is costly, however, and the experience in the 1970s suggests that there are limits to saddling public services with inexperienced and unskilled help. There is a continued need to help train the unskilled and to purchase the supportive services associated with training the poor.

3. While it is tempting to measure antipoverty efforts solely in terms of direct expenditures, the case for a federal role in family planning is a reminder that cost and effectiveness are not always synonymous. Particularly among the working poor, the size of households rather than the level of family income can be viewed as the key factor in forcing households below the poverty threshold, and programs to help the poor control the size of their families can bring major results in minimizing this trend. If a primary emphasis were placed on family planning efforts that helped the poor fulfill their own desires in reducing the number of unwanted children, at a negligible cost to the public, the next generation would have a far better chance of escaping the grasp of poverty.

4. While the efforts of the Great Society were only mildly successful in generating institutional change, the elimination of structural barriers to the advancement of the poor must remain a major component of any antipoverty strategy. The vestiges of discrimination continue to block the effective participation of minorities

150

in the American economic system, and further inhibit the self-advancement of families living in poverty. An effective campaign to reduce—and, it is hoped, obliterate—discrimination in the marketplace would not only bolster the effectiveness of other federal efforts in housing, education, and employment but also free the self-initiated energies of the vast majority of the poor who are genuinely interested in lifting themselves out of poverty. The Civil Rights Act of 1964, the Voting Rights Act of 1965, and related executive orders, if properly enforced, could prove to be more important tools to combat poverty than federal legislation involving massive investments of public funds.

In a related area, minimum wage legislation can also play a significant role in the war on poverty without large expenditures of federal resources. The use of minimum wage provisions must be limited, in that major boosts in minimum wages also tend to reduce overall employment in the private sector. The negative employment impact of higher minimum wages is impossible to measure, but prudent increases in the minimum wage can assist the plight of the working poor and reduce the inherent conflicts between transfer programs and work incentives. Protective legislation cannot be used to transform the nature of the general economy, but it can minimize its worst redistributive effects and have a major impact in promoting equal opportunity in the free market.

A MATTER OF PRIORITIES

The foregoing list of priorities omits many needs that have persuasive claims upon available resources. In some cases, omissions are justified on practical grounds. In other cases, the choices are normative. For example, this list of priorities fails to provide additional expenditures for health care. The omission reflects the judgment that the recent rapid expansion of Medicare and Medicaid has taxed available medical facilities and services. While additional health care for poor children is sorely needed, any major attempt to expand medical services to the poor further during the next few years would probably necessitate the redistribution of existing resources. The list of priorities also does not include housing improvements for the poor, even though the private housing market is woefully inadequate in providing affordable housing for low-income families.

Further improvements in benefits for the aged are also excluded from the priority agenda, in an attempt to focus on programs that strike at the roots of poverty. This is not to suggest that we can halt our present efforts in these areas, but rather that in a time of scarce resources we must channel additional federal funds in other directions.

Even in the most affluent of societies, difficult and unpleasant choices must be made among a multitude of public needs and goals. Leonard Lecht, who has carefully studied the prospects for realizing our public aspirations, concluded in his book, *The Dollar Cost of Our National Goals*, that

> we could well afford the cost of any single goal at levels reflecting current aspirations, and we could probably afford the cost for any group of goals over the next decade. We could rebuild our cities, or abolish poverty, or replace all the obsolete plants and equipment in private industry, or we could begin to develop the hardware to get us to Mars and back before the year 2000. We could make some progress on all the goals, perhaps substantial progress on many, but we cannot accomplish all our aspirations at the same time.

Clearly, priorities will have to be set among competing national goals. For a while during the Great Society period it appeared that the nation had made a commitment to eradicate poverty. Support for the drive was not sustained, however, and it is not likely that society will decide in the foreseeable future to commit resources adequate to eliminate poverty.

In the early 1980s, it is difficult to know how much additional resources our society will be willing to commit to antipoverty efforts, particularly when the problems of the poor have such a relatively low profile in the American consciousness. Given the serious inflationary pressures and critical energy shortages facing the nation, the war on poverty is not likely to achieve the preeminence that it enjoyed under the Great Society. Yet even a sustained modest annual boost in antipoverty funds would recognize the fact that the reduction of poverty remains one of several societal aspirations competing for available limited resources. This effort would result in little, if any, redistribution of income, and yet would enable us to respond gradually to the priorities outlined above, with a modest but continued effort.

As always, the willingness to commit resources to the problem of poverty is merely a reflection of its relative importance among broader national priorities. Over the past decade, the antipoverty effort has not fared well in this competition for national resources. But who can say that our priorities will change? Who would have predicted in the 1950s that poverty and hunger would be powerful issues in the following decade, or that a Republican president would advocate an expansion of the welfare system doubling the number of persons receiving assistance? One can always hope that society will undertake a truly effective, large-scale, and concerted antipoverty effort, and in so doing meet the challenge voiced by Samuel Johnson over two centuries ago: "A decent provision for the poor is the true test of civilization."

ADDITIONAL READINGS

Danziger, Sheldon, and Plotnick, Robert. *Has the War on Poverty Been Won?* New York: Academic Press, 1980.

Lecht, Leonard. *Dollars for National Goals: Looking to 1980.* New York: John Wiley & Sons, 1974.

Levitan, Sar A., and Taggart, Robert. *The Promise of Greatness.* Cambridge, Mass.: Harvard University Press, 1976.

Levitan, Sar A., and Wurzburg, Gregory. *Evaluating Federal Social Programs: An Uncertain Art.* Kalamazoo, Mich.: The W.E. Upjohn Institute for Employment Research, 1979.

Schorr, Alvin L. *Jubilee for Our Times; A Practical Program for Income Equality.* New York: Columbia University Press, 1977.

DISCUSSION QUESTIONS

1. How would you evaluate the legacy of the Great Society?
2. "We stand at the edge of the greatest era in the life of any nation. For the first time in world history, we have the abundance and the ability to free every man from hopeless want, and to free every person to find fulfillment in the works of his mind or the labor of his hands.

   This nation, this people, this generation, has man's first chance to create a Great Society: a society of success without squalor, beauty without barrenness, works of genius without the wretchedness of poverty."

   —Lyndon B. Johnson, June 26, 1964

What do you think prevented the realization of President Johnson's vision?

3. What would be your prescription for alleviating poverty in the United States? What would be your order of priorities?

4. "The welfare state is driving the nation to the poorhouse." Evaluate this charge in light of the experience over the past two decades.

5. You are informed that there will be no additional funds for employment and welfare programs during the coming year. If more funds are needed for specific programs, they will have to come from "savings" in other ongoing welfare efforts.

   a. What programs would you cut, if any?

   b. What programs would you expand with the funds saved from the retrenchments?

   c. Would you transfer "savings" to nonwelfare programs or reduce the federal budget deficit?

   (No rhetoric, please, about cutting defense. Any cuts must be made from welfare and employment programs. That's a nonnegotiable condition for the purpose of this exercise.)

Index